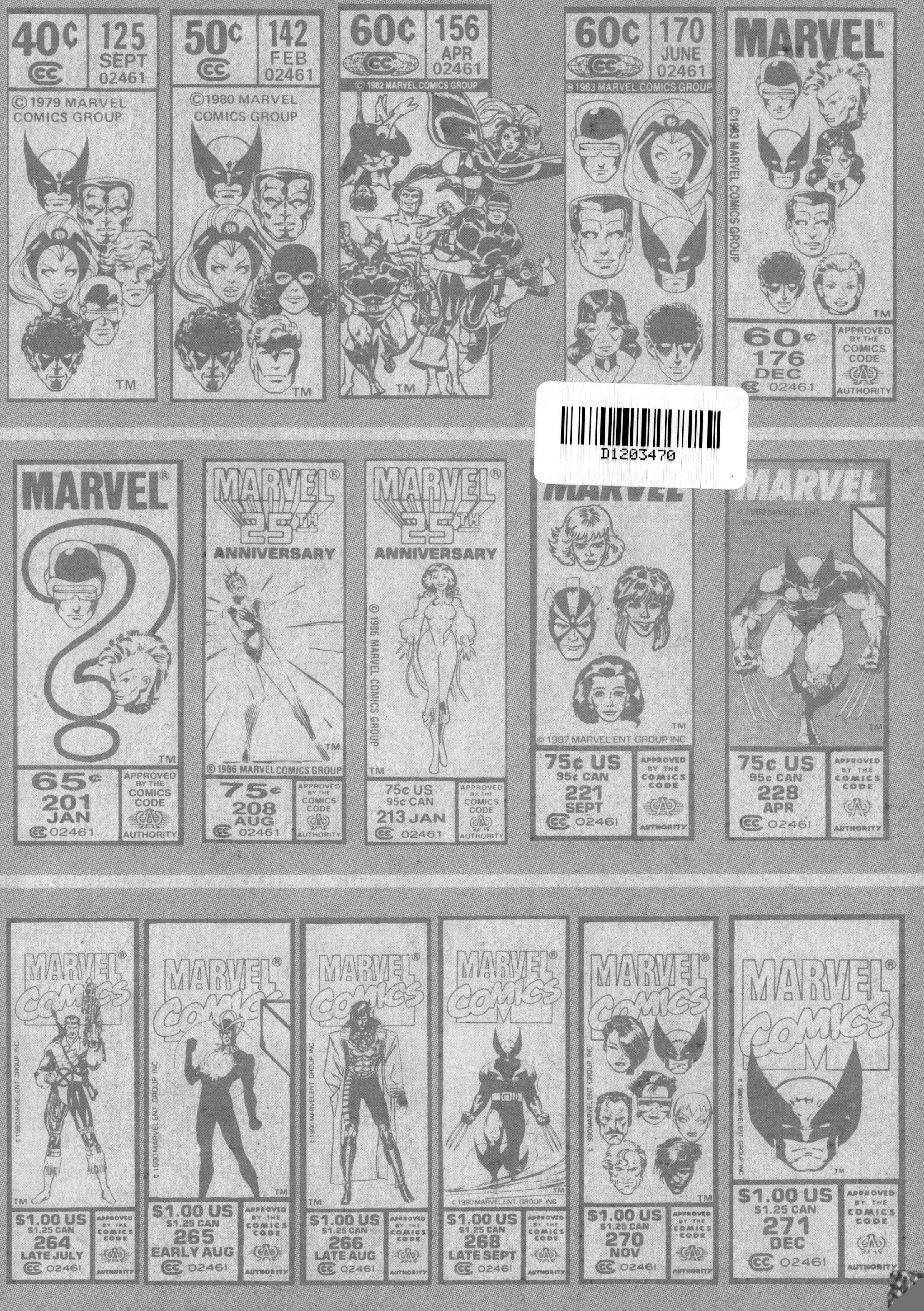
40¢
125
SEPT
02461
© 1979 MARVEL COMICS GROUP
TM
50¢
142
FEB
02461
© 1980 MARVEL COMICS GROUP
TM
60¢
156
APR
02461
© 1982 MARVEL COMICS GROUP
TM
60¢
170
JUNE
02461
© 1983 MARVEL COMICS GROUP
MARVEL®
© 1983 MARVEL COMICS GROUP
TM
60¢
176
DEC
02461
APPROVED BY THE COMICS CODE AUTHORITY
D1203470
MARVEL®
TM
65¢
201
JAN
02461
APPROVED BY THE COMICS CODE AUTHORITY
MARVEL® 25TH ANNIVERSARY
TM
© 1986 MARVEL COMICS GROUP
75¢
208
AUG
02461
APPROVED BY THE COMICS CODE AUTHORITY
MARVEL® 25TH ANNIVERSARY
© 1986 MARVEL COMICS GROUP
TM
75¢ US
95¢ CAN
213 JAN
02461
APPROVED BY THE COMICS CODE AUTHORITY
MARVEL
TM
© 1987 MARVEL ENT. GROUP INC.
75¢ US
95¢ CAN
221
SEPT
02461
APPROVED BY THE COMICS CODE AUTHORITY
MARVEL
TM
75¢ US
95¢ CAN
228
APR
02461
APPROVED BY THE COMICS CODE AUTHORITY
MARVEL® COMICS
© 1990 MARVEL ENT. GROUP INC.
TM
$1.00 US
$1.25 CAN
264
LATE JULY
02461
APPROVED BY THE COMICS CODE AUTHORITY
MARVEL® COMICS
© 1990 MARVEL ENT. GROUP INC.
TM
$1.00 US
$1.25 CAN
265
EARLY AUG
02461
APPROVED BY THE COMICS CODE AUTHORITY
MARVEL® COMICS
© 1990 MARVEL ENT. GROUP INC.
TM
$1.00 US
$1.25 CAN
266
LATE AUG
02461
APPROVED BY THE COMICS CODE AUTHORITY
MARVEL® COMICS
TM
© 1990 MARVEL ENT. GROUP INC.
$1.00 US
$1.25 CAN
268
LATE SEPT
02461
APPROVED BY THE COMICS CODE AUTHORITY
MARVEL® COMICS
© 1990 MARVEL ENT. GROUP INC.
TM
$1.00 US
$1.25 CAN
270
NOV
02461
APPROVED BY THE COMICS CODE AUTHORITY
MARVEL® COMICS
© 1990 MARVEL ENT. GROUP INC.
TM
$1.00 US
$1.25 CAN
271
DEC
02461
APPROVED BY THE COMICS CODE AUTHORITY

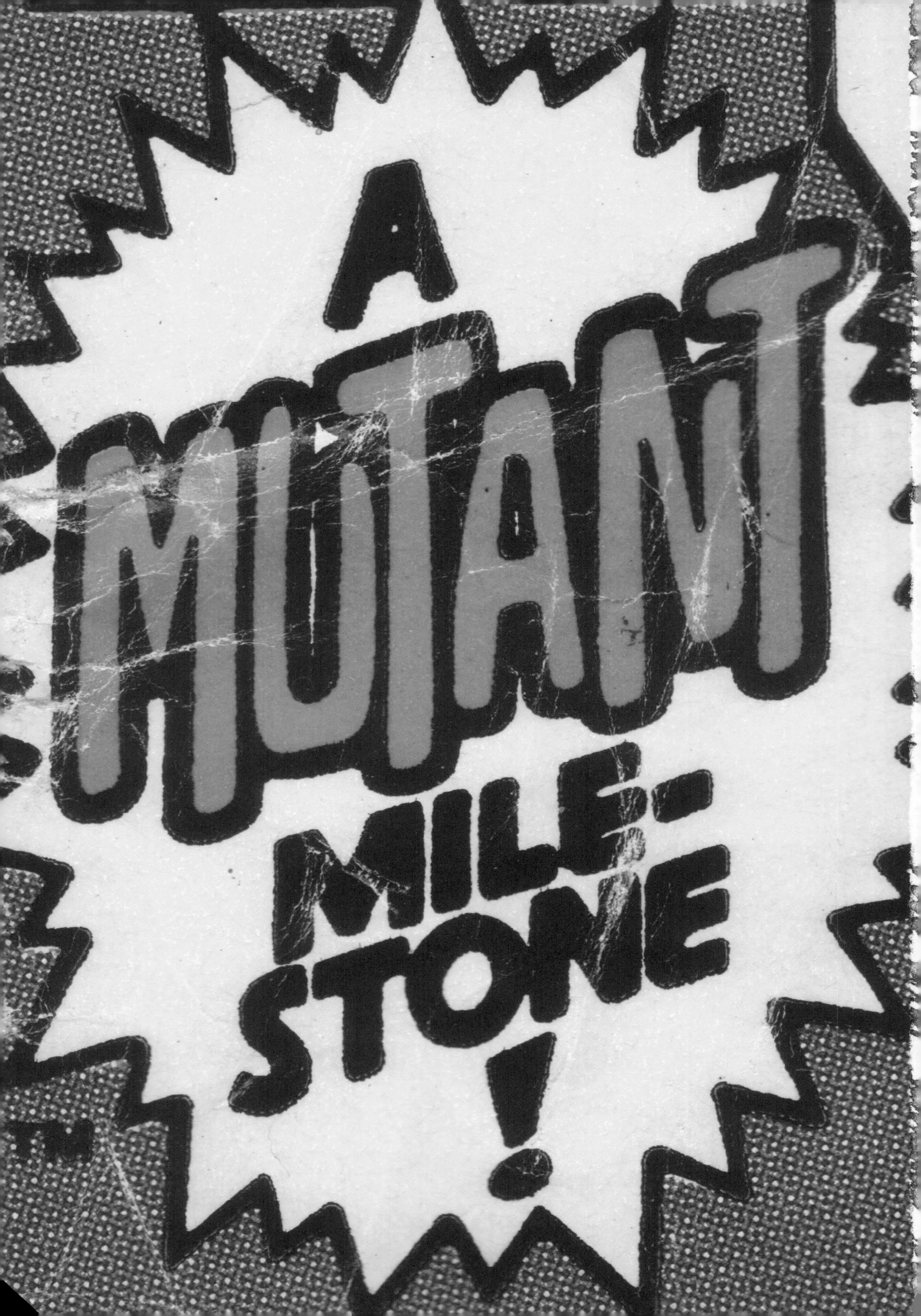
A MUTANT MILE-STONE!

X-MEN
GRAND DESIGN

BY

ED PISKOR

A MARVEL COMIC

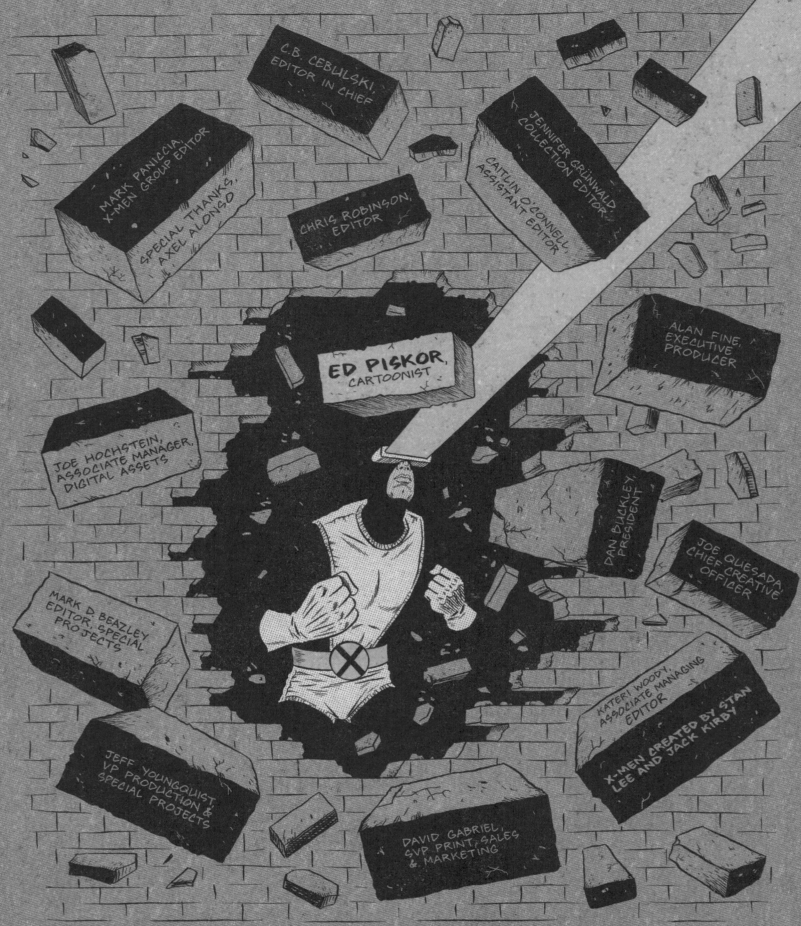

X-MEN: GRAND DESIGN. CONTAINS MATERIAL ORIGINALLY PUBLISHED IN MAGAZINE FORM AS X-MEN: GRAND DESIGN #1-2. FIRST PRINTING 2018. ISBN# 978-1-302-90489-0. PUBLISHED BY MARVEL WORLDWIDE, INC., A SUBSIDIARY OF MARVEL ENTERTAINMENT, LLC. OFFICE OF PUBLICATION: 135 WEST 50TH STREET, NEW YORK, NY 10020. COPYRIGHT © 2018 MARVEL NO SIMILARITY BETWEEN ANY OF THE NAMES, CHARACTERS, PERSONS, AND/OR INSTITUTIONS IN THIS MAGAZINE WITH THOSE OF ANY LIVING OR DEAD PERSON OR INSTITUTION IS INTENDED, AND ANY SIMILARITY WHICH MAY EXIST IS PURELY COINCIDENTAL. PRINTED IN CANADA. DAN BUCKLEY, PRESIDENT, MARVEL ENTERTAINMENT; JOE QUESADA, CHIEF CREATIVE OFFICER; TOM BREEVORT, SVP OF PUBLISHING; DAVID BOGART, SVP OF BUSINESS AFFAIRS AND OPERATIONS, PUBLISHING & PARTNERSHIP; DAVID GABRIEL, SVP OF SALES & MARKETING, PUBLISHING; JEFF YOUNGQUIST, VP OF PRODUCTION & SPECIAL PROJECTS; DAN CARR, EXECUTIVE DIRECTOR OF PUBLISHING TECHNOLOGY; ALEX MORALES, DIRECTOR OF PUBLISHING OPERATIONS; SUSAN CRESPI, PRODUCTION MANAGER; STAN LEE, CHAIRMAN EMERITUS. FOR INFORMATION REGARDING ADVERTISING IN MARVEL COMICS OR ON MARVEL.COM, PLEASE CONTACT VIT DeBELLIS, INTEGRATED SALES MANAGER AT VDEBELLIS@MARVEL.COM. FOR MARVEL SUBSCRIPTION INQUIRIES, PLEASE CALL 888-511-5480.

MANUFACTURED BETWEEN 1/26/2018 AND 2/27/2018 BY FRIESENS, ALTONA, MB, CANADA.

10 9 8 7 6 5 4 3 2 1

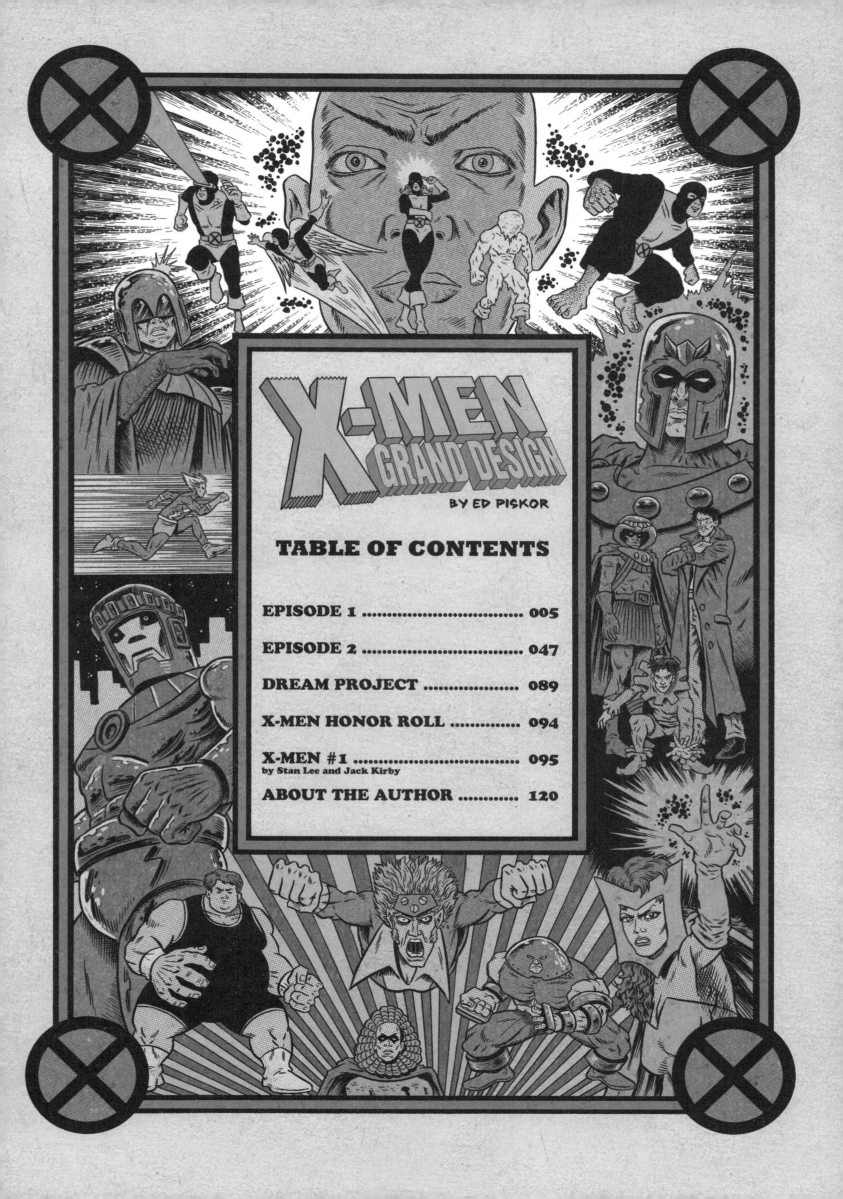

X-MEN GRAND DESIGN

BY ED PISKOR

TABLE OF CONTENTS

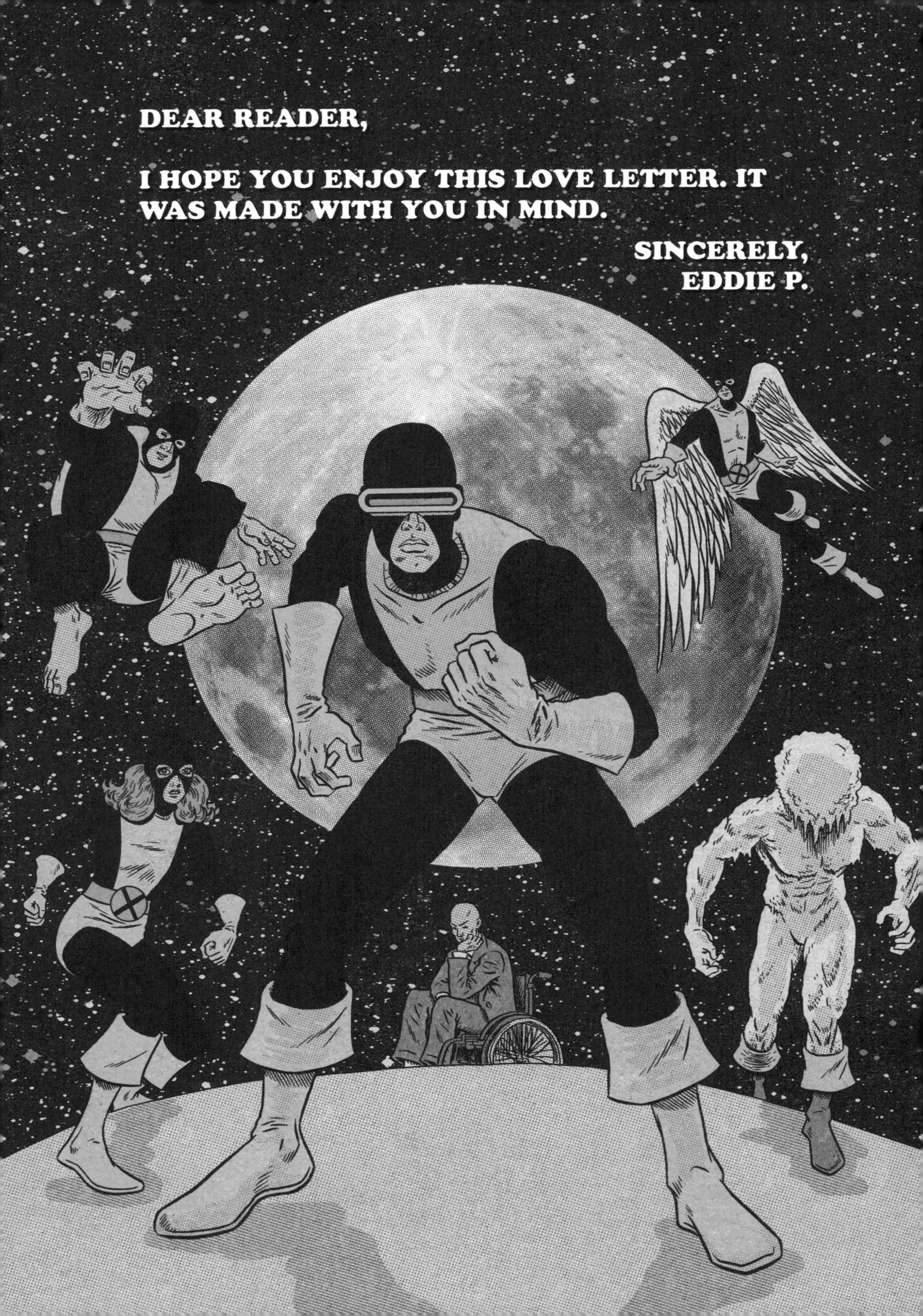
DEAR READER,
I HOPE YOU ENJOY THIS LOVE LETTER. IT WAS MADE WITH YOU IN MIND.
SINCERELY,
EDDIE P.

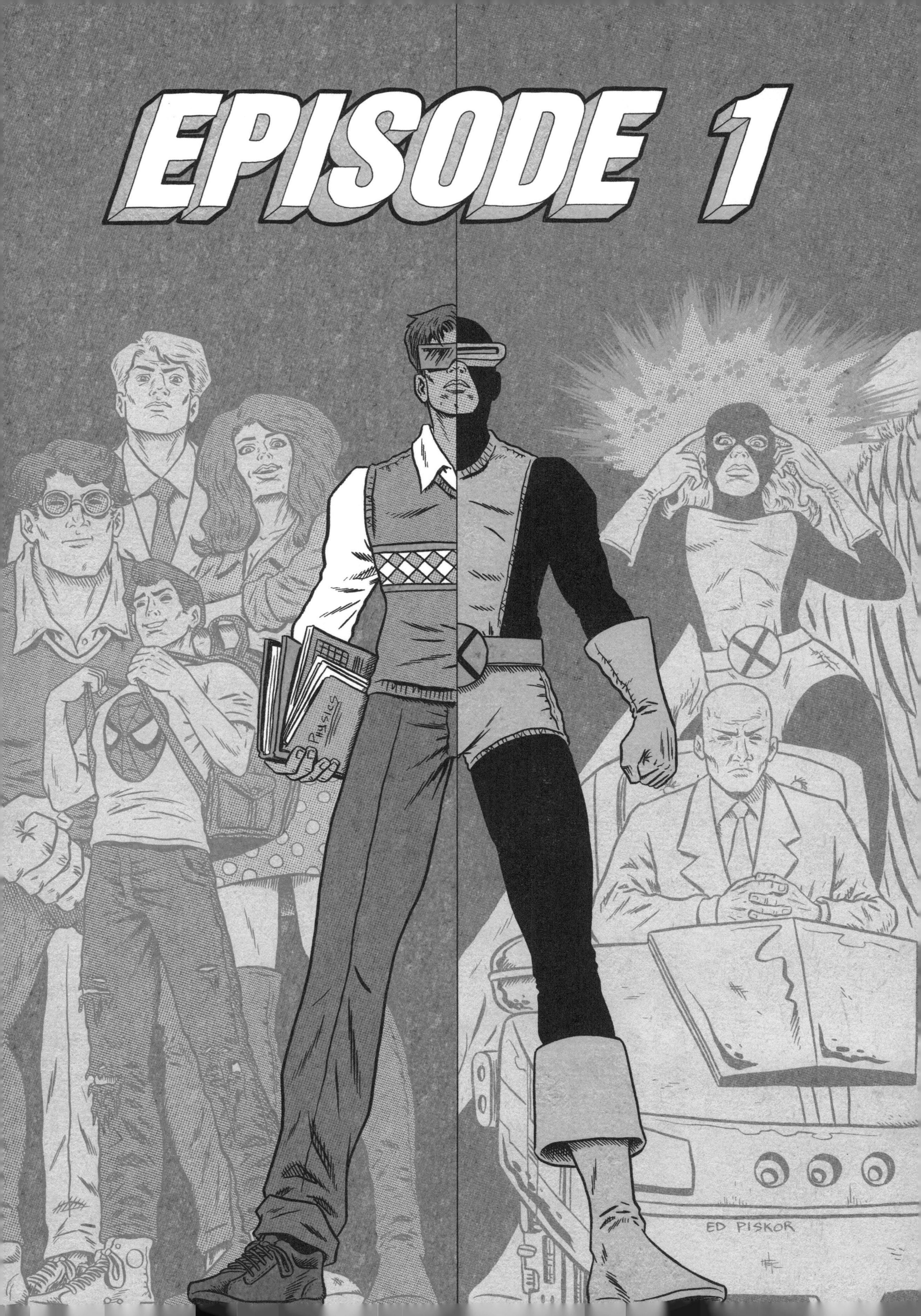
EPISODE 1
PHYSICS
ED PISKOR

RECORDER. I'M READY FOR YOU...

PERFECT TIMING, WATCHER. ETERNITY HAS BEEN CONCERNED ABOUT YOUR PRODUCTIVITY.

I'VE LEARNED OVER SEVERAL MILLENNIA THAT IT IS NECESSARY FOR EVENTS TO UNFOLD AND SETTLE BEFORE TRANSCRIBING WHAT I WITNESS.

THERE WERE MANY MECHANISMS AT PLAY WITH THESE PARTICULAR SUBJECTS. MUCH I NEEDED TO DIGEST AND MAKE SENSE OF.

AT THIS MOMENT, I FINALLY UNDERSTAND IT ALL IN A CLEAR MANNER. YOU MAY BEGIN RECORDING.

3... 2... 1...

BOOP!

I'LL NOW DISCLOSE EVERYTHING I'VE OBSERVED ABOUT A VERY EXTRAORDINARY PANTHEON OF MUTANTS...

"MUTANT" IS OFTEN VERBALIZED AS A PEJORATIVE TERM, EVEN THOUGH THE VERY BASIS OF HUMAN EVOLUTION REQUIRES MUTATION FOR ADAPTING TO NEW, HARSH CONDITIONS.

HA HA!

HEH HA!!

VILE CREATURE!

FEH! DISGUSTING!

AW, MA, WHY CAN'T **JIMMY** EVER COME OVER TO OUR HOUSE TO PLAY?

FOR THE SAKE OF SELF-PRESERVATION, GENETICALLY MUTATED "PARA-HUMANS" WOULD ROUTINELY OVEREXTEND THEMSELVES TO KEEP IN THE GOOD GRACES OF THE MASSES.

THANKS, JEREMIAH!

NO PROBLEM AT ALL ...

COME HERE, YOU BAD GIRL!

MAKE SURE YOU WASH YOUR HANDS WHEN WE GO IN-SIDE!

THE TENSION BETWEEN HUMANS AND MUTANTS WAS PALPABLE FOR CENTURIES, BUT PREJUDICES LARGELY REMAINED UNDER THE SURFACE, UNTIL ONE FATEFUL DAY IN THE 1900S WHEN EVERYONE'S WORST NIGHTMARES WERE REALIZED.

IN JUST A FEW HOURS THE NOTORIOUS MUTANT **NAMOR THE SUB-MARINER** WAS RESPONSIBLE FOR KILLING TENS OF THOUSANDS AND DISPLACING MILLIONS IN THE HEART OF **NEW YORK CITY**.

EXTREME FEAR SEEMS TO HAVE EASE IN BLURRING THE VISION OF OTHERWISE REASONABLE PEOPLE.

DEATH TO MUTIES!

GIT OUTTA 'MERICA!

8

ON THE **50TH** NIGHT **NEW YORK** REMAINED SUBMERGED UNDERWATER, THE IDEALISTIC HEROES OF THE TIME CONCEDED THAT THERE WERE NO MORE **SURVIVORS** TO LOCATE AND THEIR MISSION **TRANSFORMED...**

NO, THIS ISN'T HIM, EITHER.

AW SHUCKS...

FIN, WE NEED TO QUESTION EVERY STRAY **ATLANTEAN** YOU CAN FIND DOWN THERE UNTIL WE GET OUR PERPETRATOR!

AYE-AYE, **ANGEL.**

NO PERSON OR ORGANIZATION COULD FIGURE OUT HOW TO DIVERT THE PUTRID, STAGNANT, POISONOUS WATER FROM THE CITY UNTIL A PAIR OF SCIENTISTS, **SHARON** AND **BRIAN XAVIER**, DEVELOPED A TECHNOLOGICAL SOLUTION TO THIS CATASTROPHE.

IT ONLY TOOK A FEW DAYS TO DRY OUT THE AREA, BUT IT TOOK MORE THAN A DECADE TO GET **NEW YORK CITY** BACK INTO SHAPE.

ONE WAY

THE **XAVIERS'** GENIUS WAS HANDSOMELY REWARDED WHEN THE WEAPONS MANUFACTURER **STARK INDUSTRIES** BOUGHT THEIR TECHNOLOGY AND KEPT THEM ON RETAINER.

A BABY?!

I THINK WE HAVE ROOM FOR ONE MORE. HA!

THE **UNITED STATES** GOVERNMENT SOON COMMISSIONED **STARK** ON A PROJECT TO SPLIT THE ATOM FOR MILITARY PURPOSES. THE FIRST PHONE CALL **HOWARD STARK** MADE WAS TO THE **XAVIERS.**

DESPITE ALL THEIR INTELLIGENCE, THE YOUNG COUPLE NEVER CONSIDERED THE EFFECT THAT THEIR WORK ENVIRONMENT WOULD HAVE ON THEIR OFFSPRING.

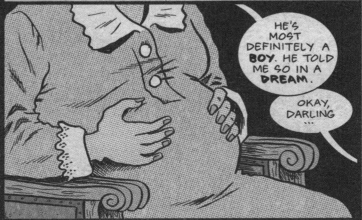

HE'S MOST DEFINITELY A **BOY.** HE TOLD ME SO IN A **DREAM.**

OKAY, DARLING...

WITHOUT EVEN BRINGING **MUTANTS** INTO THE EQUATION, **HUMANITY** HAS HAD NO TROUBLE FINDING CONFLICT AMONGST EACH OTHER. EVERY GENERATION SEEMS TO DEFINE THEMSELVES BY THE WARS OF THEIR ERA.

<PLEASE, STOP!>*

LOGAN, DON'T...

* TRANSLATED FROM **GERMAN**.

...WE CAN'T BLOW OUR COVER JUST YET.

THAT'S A KID THEY'RE HOUNDIN'!

WHA?

BOP

CRAK

BOOP

POW

POP

DINK

NOK

OOF

BOOF

POK

WHAT GIVES, CAP'N?

I... I DON'T KNOW...

MY **SHIELD**... IT WAS **RIPPED** FROM MY ARM...

WHERE'D THE BOY DISAPPEAR TO?

>Sniff<
>Sniff<

THE ARMS RACE TO THE **ATOMIC BOMB** COST MORE THAN JUST MANPOWER AND MONEY.

BRIAN!

BRIAN XAVIER LEAVES BEHIND A SON, **CHARLES**, WHO ALREADY MISSES THEIR LATE, NIGHT ICE CREAM SESSIONS AND THE SMELLS THAT ACCOMPANY A FATHER AFTER A HARD DAY'S WORK.

WHEN **DR. KURT MARKO** AND HIS SON MOVED INTO THE **XAVIER** MANSION A YEAR OR SO LATER, THEIR COLLEAGUES FROM THE **MANHATTAN PROJECT** WARNED **SHARON**. MARKO WAS A HARD MAN TO READ FOR EVERYBODY EXCEPT YOUNG **CHARLES**.

CHARLES, HONEY, COME SHOW YOUR NEW BROTHER HIS BEDROOM.

YES, MOMMY.

THE STRESS OF THEIR FIRST OFFICIAL DAY TOGETHER AS A FAMILY TRIGGERED SOMETHING IN THE **XAVIER** BOY.

CAIN MARKO, YOU APOLOGIZE THIS INSTANT!

...BUT HIS SKINNY NECK **DOES** MAKE HIS HEAD LOOK LIKE A LOLLIPOP!

CHARLES COULD HEAR **DR. MARKO'S** MIND, AND THE MAN'S THOUGHTS WERE IN A MISGUIDED, BUT HONEST, PLACE. **KURT** TRULY BELIEVED THAT A MOTHER FIGURE WOULD BE THE MIRACLE HIS POOR **CAIN** WOULD NEED TO BECOME A STABLE, WELL-ADJUSTED BOY.

MAGNUS WASN'T SURE HOW HE WAS ABLE TO EVADE CAPTURE BY POSSESSING **CAPTAIN AMERICA'S** SHIELD...

HE WONDERS, IF HE TRIED HARD ENOUGH, COULD HE DO IT AGAIN. THEN HE DOESN'T DO MUCH THINK- ING AT ALL...

HE COULDN'T DISCERN WHETHER HE WAS COMATOSE FOR HOURS, DAYS OR WEEKS.

AFTER REGAINING HIS SENSES, **MAGNUS** CHARTED THE MONTHS OF HIS INCARCERATION BY SCRATCHING A METAL NAIL INTO HIS PLYWOOD SLEEPING AREA.

EACH NIGHT HE WOULD WAIT LATE ENOUGH FOR EVERY- ONE TO SLEEP SO THAT HE COULD TRACK HIS PROGRESS WITHOUT EVER TOUCHING THAT NAIL.

THE **NAZIS** WOULD FALL INTO A PREDICTABLE ROUTINE WHEN TIME PASSED WITHOUT INCIDENT.

MAGNUS DISCOVERED IT ACTUALLY WASN'T THAT DIFFICULT TO COMMAND AND CONTROL FERROUS METALS AFTER PLENTY OF PRACTICE.

< KEEP SILENT, MAGDA ...>

EVERYBODY THOUGHT **CHARLES XAVIER'S** NEW HOMELIFE WAS THE CAUSE OF HIS POOR PERFORMANCE IN SCHOOL...

I WONDER IF GINNY LIKES ME? IS THIS A PIMPLE? OH NO. IF HE FIGHTS ME NEAR THE NEIGHBORHOOD I'LL GET MY BIGGER BROTHER TO HELP. WHO YOU LOOKING AT? THAT IS SO HORRIBLE. YOU WORE THE SAME DRESS AS ME ON PURPOSE. IF MRS. PARKER GAVE ME THE CHANCE. AW, FORGET IT. SIXTEEN TOMORROW! SHOULD I USE THE TOILET HERE OR WAIT UNTIL I GET HOME? HOW CAN I THINK ABOUT MATH WITH JENNY SITTING IN FRONT OF ME LIKE THIS? SOMEDAY I'LL BE BOSS. THAT WILL SHOW THEM. DOES HE SEE MY FRECKLES? I DON'T THINK ANYBODY ELSE SMELLED IT. PHEW. IF MY DAD KNEW I DIDN'T STAND UP TO SALUTE THE FLAG THIS MORNING. I CAN'T BELIEVE JACOB. WHAT A DUMMY. HOW CAN SHE JUST WALK BY ME LIKE THAT? MY EYES AREN'T GRAY, THEY'RE GREEN. THAT'S PRETTY FUN. DID HE JUST PUT HIS LIPS ON THE WATER FOUNTAIN? HOW DID HE HAVE THE CONFIDENCE TO ASK FOR HER NUMBER LIKE THAT? BALD KID'S A FREAK! SO WEIRD. WHAT'S HIS PROBLEM?

IT PROVED TO BE MORE PRODUCTIVE ACADEMICALLY FOR THE BOY TO IMMERSE HIMSELF AT HOME IN AN AUTODIDACTIC FASHION.

IF **CHARLES** EVER LET HIS GUARD DOWN, THE DREAMS, NIGHTMARES, AND FANTASIES OF HIS FAMILY WOULD SEEP INTO HIS OWN SUBCONSCIOUS.

MMMM. YOU'RE A GENTLEMAN. THANK YOU VERY MUCH FOR THE ROSE. HOW MUCH? WASN'T HARD TO KILL BRIAN... CHARLES GOT A TOUCHDOWN! A SAILOR, YOU SAID? MY... WELL, SURE. MUSHROOMS? CHUPACABRA BONES! THIS IS A JOB FOR KURT THE FLIRT. YOU'RE ADORABLE. WHAT ABOUT YOUR WIFE? WHAT WIFE? OH KURT! DON'T NEED ANOTHER RING. WHAT'S THE... IS... IS THAT A OM... FIRSTER. A FIDE... TO MANAG... PROBLEM. WOULD BE... MATERIAL H... WH... CAN W...

IRONICALLY, THE ONLY TIME THAT **CHARLES** COULD COUNT ON BEING FREE FROM **CAIN MARKO'S** DEMENTED MIND WAS DURING THOSE LATE NIGHTS...

DON'T TURN THIS ROBBERY INTO A MURDER.

WHEN **CAIN** WAS AT **XAVIER MANSION**, HE HAD A SINGLE PREOCCUPATION IN **CHARLES'** FAVORITE ROOM.

WE TRIED EVERYTHING TO GET IN THERE, CAIN.

NOT "EVERYTHING" UNTIL WE TRY LIQUID ADAMANTIUM.

CHARLES XAVIER'S SECOND FAVORITE ROOM WAS THE LABORATORY IN THE SUB-BASEMENT WHERE HIS PARENTS WOULD SHOW THE BOYS ALL MANNER OF ALCHEMY.

I THINK I REMEMBER HOW IT GOES.

THE ESTATE RESTED AT THE NORTHEASTERN TIP OF **WESTCHESTER** COUNTY, **NEW YORK**, ABOUT 40 MINUTES AWAY FROM THE NEAREST FIRST RESPONDERS.

MOM!

WAKE UP, MOM!!

≥KOFF!

CHARLES DIDN'T HAVE TO READ THE FIREFIGHTER'S THOUGHTS TO KNOW WHAT HE WAS ABOUT TO SAY.

SOMETHING DEEP IN **CHARLES XAVIER'S** REPTILIAN BRAIN WISHED THAT **CAIN MARKO** PERISHED THAT NIGHT WITH THE REST.

THIS DARKNESS PROMPTED **XAVIER** TO SEARCH THE WORLD FOR ASSISTANCE IN CALMING THE VOICES WITHIN HIS MIND.

CHARLES HEARD TELL THAT THERE WAS ANOTHER LIKE HIM.

IT TOOK YEARS FOR **CHARLES** TO EVER SPEAK ABOUT HIS DETOUR THROUGH **CAIRO, EGYPT.**

WHOA, THERE...

HEY!

THAT GIRL... MY WALLET... STOP!

GOOD LITTLE RAT. HA HA HA HA...

HA HA HA HA HA HA HA!

WHO ARE YOU?

WHAT ARE YOU DOING TO THIS CHILD?

THE RAT HAS SERVED ITS PURPOSE.

YOU SHOULDN'T HAVE COME HERE, STRANGER...

YOUR MIND TELLS ME MUCH...

YOU CUT ME FROM YOUR THOUGHTS? I DON'T LIKE THAT.

ENOUGH...

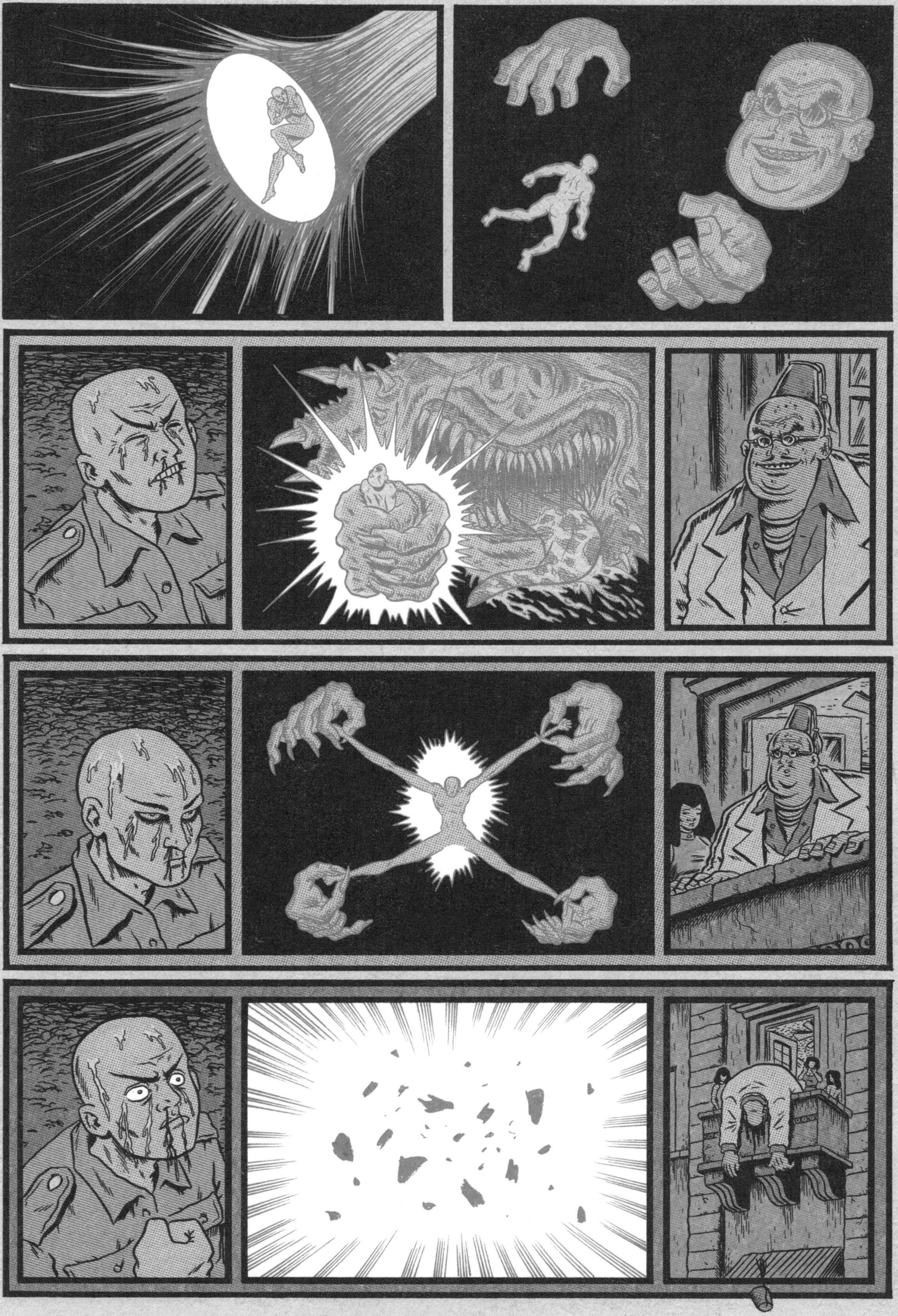

IT TOOK TIME, RESOURCEFULNESS, AND HARD WORK, BUT **MAGNUS** AND **MAGDA** BUILT A TOLERABLE LIFE TOGETHER AFTER THEY GOT THE STENCH OF THE CAMPS OUT OF THEIR PORES.

...MAGNUS!

IT'S BEEN A YEAR AND STILL NOBODY WILL SPEAK TO ME...

OF COURSE, THIS DOESN'T MEAN THEY'LL EVER BE ABLE TO FORGET THE ATROCITIES.

THEY TURN THEIR NOSES UP AT ME... AT YOUR DAUGHTER!

WE'RE STILL NEW TO THIS COMMUNITY. THEY'RE A VERY PRIVATE PEOPLE...

MAGNUS HAS NO REAL TRADE, BUT HE WOULD BREAK HIS BACK TO PROVIDE FOR HIS FAMILY, AND THE TOWNSPEOPLE KNOW IT.

BUT, SIR, THIS IS ONLY HALF THE PAY THAT YOU PROMISED?!

BAH! IT'S PLENTY FOR **YOU!**

BUT... **BUT, PLEASE!!** PLEASE DON'T WALK AWAY, SIR. **SIR!!**

PLEASE JUST PAY ME WHAT YOU PROMISED, SIR...

YES... YES, I'LL PAY...

HEY, WHAT IS THIS?

THE OTHER FARMHANDS TOOK QUICK CONSENSUS AND DECIDED **MAGNUS** MUST BE A WARLOCK.

BY THE TIME HE WAS ABLE TO SCRAPE HIMSELF OUT OF THE MUD AND HEAD HOME...

MAGDA...

ANYA...

NO...

HOW IS IT STILL ALIVE?

UNGODLY CREATURE...

GET YOUR KNIFE, ELIAS.

YES...

IF WE DON'T TAKE ITS HEAD OFF...

...IT WILL HAUNT THE VILLAGE ETERNALLY...

YES...

HERE, ELIAS...

...COME SLIT ITS THROAT...

YES.

THERE ARE ABOUT THREE TO FOUR GRAMS OF **IRON** WITHIN THE HUMAN BODY. THIS SMALL AMOUNT OF METAL WORKS OVERTIME, SHUTTLING OXYGEN THROUGHOUT A PERSON'S FRAMEWORK...

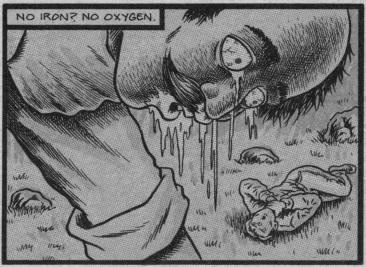

NO IRON? NO OXYGEN.

CHARLES XAVIER KNEW WHEN HIS BOOTS TOUCHED AMERICAN SOIL THAT HE'D IMMEDIATELY BE DRAFTED INTO THE MILITARY FOR A WAR HE HAD NO INTEREST IN. HE HAD THE MONEY AND CONNECTIONS TO EVADE, BUT DIDN'T BOTHER.

X, MAN, THAT SNIPER HAD US DEAD TO RIGHTS. HOW'D YOU KNOW WHERE HE WAS?

JUST A FEELING, SIR...

HE WASN'T EXPECTING TO GET LUMPED INTO THE SAME PLATOON AS HIS STEPBROTHER, CAIN MARKO.

I NEVER THOUGHT YOU HAD IT IN YA...

HA HA... IZZAT HIS BRAINS COMIN' OUTTA HIS EARS?

ON ONE FATEFUL DAY, THE BROTHERS WERE SIMPLY TASKED WITH LOCATING HIDDEN ENEMY WEAPONS CACHES...

THEY ENDED UP IN PERHAPS THE LAST PIECE OF EARTH DEVOID OF EVER HAVING HUMAN CONTACT, THOUGH SOMETHING ELSE HAD SURELY BEEN THERE...

CAIN! LET IT BE!

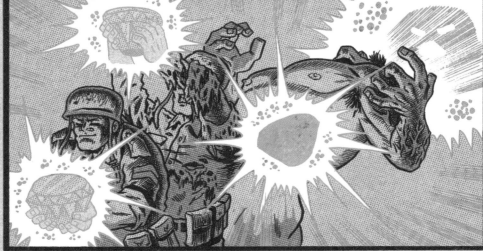

CAIN!

CAIN MARKO'S BODY WAS NEVER RECOVERED FROM THE HIDDEN TEMPLE OF CYTTORAK...

CHARLES WAS LUCKY, BUT HE DIDN'T WALK AWAY UNSCATHED.

NOW THAT CHARLES IS NO LONGER AN EFFECTIVE MILITARY SPECIMEN, HE BEGINS INVESTING TIME INTO A PROJECT THAT WOULD PROBABLY GET HIM BRANDED A **SEDITIOUS TERRORIST** IF IT WERE EVER DISCOVERED.

"I LOST MY WHOLE FAMILY WHEN I WAS YOUNG BECAUSE OF **NAMOR**. I JUST DON'T WANT ANY MORE TRAGEDY... FOR ANYBODY."

"WHAT IF WE MAKE A **MUTIE** MAD ENOUGH? WHAT IF THE **FANTASTIC FOUR** OR **AVENGERS** ARE BUSY WHEN A **GENE-JOKE** GOES OFF THE RAILS?"

"... MANDATORY DNA TESTING WHEN DOCTORS ACCEPT NEW PATIENTS! SNIFF THEM SNEAKY **MUTANTS** OUT!"

XAVIER HASN'T BEEN **OUTED** AS A **MUTANT**, BUT HE'S **DEFINITELY** BEING WATCHED.

REGISTRATION!

MUTANT LOVE

MUTANTS ARE PEOPLE TOO

IT WAS AT A MUTANTS' **RIGHTS DEMONSTRATION** THAT HE MET HER...

WOW! WHO IS THIS?

MOIRA MacTAGGERT, ASPIRING PhD IN THE FIELD OF **MUTANT RESEARCH AND GENETICS**...

HUH?

OOPS...

MOIRA'S THESIS CONTAINS RARE INFORMATION ABOUT MUTANT PHYSIOLOGY, WHICH COULD BE THE KEY INGREDIENT FOR **CHARLES'** SECRET DEVICE.

HOW'D YE DO THAT?

IN ABOUT TWO MONTHS THE COUPLE BECOMES IN-SEPARABLE, AND **XAVIER'S** PROJECT BECOMES A SHARED SECRET THAT IS NOW READY TO TEST.

COULDN'T HAVE DONE THIS WITH-OUT YOU, MOIRA...

STAY OUT OF MY MIND, CHARLES.

CEREBRO, A COMPUTER BUILT TO AMPLIFY **CHARLES'** MENTAL POWER IN AID OF LOCATING FELLOW **MUTANTS**.

BE BACK SOON, **MY LOVE**...

AT THE FLICK OF A SWITCH, **XAVIER** IMMEDIATELY BECOMES LESS LONELY ON THIS TINY GLOBE.

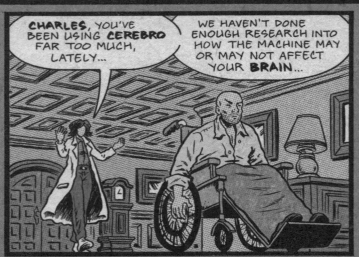

CHARLES, YOU'VE BEEN USING **CEREBRO** FAR TOO MUCH, LATELY...

WE HAVEN'T DONE ENOUGH RESEARCH INTO HOW THE MACHINE MAY OR MAY NOT AFFECT YOUR **BRAIN**...

THERE'S PLENTY OF DATA FOR US TO BEGIN REACHING OUT TO **MUTANTS** YOU'VE ALREADY DISCOVERED...

THE VOLUME OF **MUTANTS** OUT THERE, **MOIRA**. THE **VARIETY**. EACH WITH A UNIQUE **POWER** OR **ABILITY**...

...I MUST FIND MUTANTS WITH THE SAME POTENTIAL AS THAT **MONSTER** THAT I ENCOUNTERED IN **EGYPT**...

WE CAN SAVE THEM FROM GETTING CONSUMED BY THEIR POWERS IF WE CAN GET TO THEM EARLY IN THEIR DEVELOPMENT.

MOIRA, MOIRA!

I'VE GOT ONE!

...A MUTANT OFF THE CHARTS... HE'S GOING TO BE... MOIRA?

SCOTLAND?!

20

XAVIER ESCAPED HIS PERSONAL LOSSES BY TRAVELING TO ISRAEL, HOPING THAT HE COULD PUT HIS PSYCHIC ABILITIES TO GOOD USE WHILE SUPRESSING HIS EMOTIONS ALONG THE WAY.

DR. XAVIER. YOUR REPUTATION PRECEDES YOU.

HA! WELL, I'LL DO MY BEST.

HE DIDN'T RANDOMLY CHOOSE THIS DESTINATION...

THANK YOU, MAGNUS.

CHARLES, THIS IS GABRIELLE HALLER. SHE'S OUR MOST SEVERE CASE OF CATATONIC SCHIZOPHRENIA...

MANY OF THE HOSPITAL'S STAFF AND PATIENTS SURVIVED THE CONCENTRATION CAMPS DURING THE WAR.

THE TREATMENT WAS EXHAUSTIVE FOR CHARLES. LOTS OF MENTAL BARRIERS TO TRAVERSE BEFORE THE REAL WORK BEGINS...

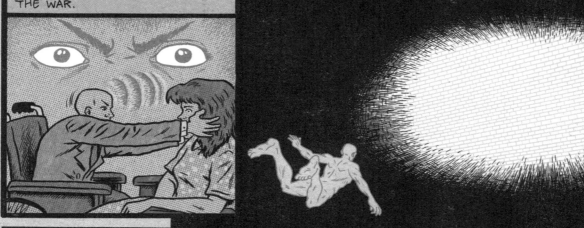

WHEN THE DEMONS WERE CONQUERED, IT ALL BE-CAME WORTH IT.

MOM...

DADDY?

IT TOOK A FEW WEEKS BEFORE CHARLES COULD CATCH THE ORDERLY WITHOUT INTERRUPTION.

MAGNUS?

THIRSTY?

...I DISAGREE, **MAGNUS**. IT IS VERY POSSIBLE FOR HUMANS AND MUTANTS TO COEXIST. I DON'T DENY THERE IS MORE WORK TO BE DONE. HARD WORK.

NONSENSE...

WHEN IT BECOMES POLITICALLY AND LEGALLY PERMISSABLE, THEY WILL DOOM US TO EXTINCTION IN SOME FORM OR FASHION.

I'VE SEEN IT HAPPEN BEFORE...

WHAT OTHER OPTION IS OUT THERE BUT LIVING SIDE-BY-SIDE IN PEACE?

WORLD DOMINATION.

HA HA HA HA.

GOOD ONE, **MAGNUS**.

EVEN WITH TWO STRONG ARMIES, IT LOOKS LIKE WE HAVE A **STALEMATE**, CHARLES...

CHARLES, TELL ME WHAT HAS CHANGED BETWEEN US? WHAT IS WRONG?

I'VE DONE WRONG BY YOU, GABRIELLE...

...YOU WERE MY PATIENT. I WAS INSIDE YOUR MIND. I **INVADED** YOUR THOUGHTS.

COULD I HAVE LEFT SOMETHING BEHIND? DID I PLANT THE FEELINGS YOU HAVE TOWARD ME?

I DON'T KNOW WHAT I'VE DONE. I DON'T KNOW WHAT I'M CAPABLE OF. I **BETRAYED** YOU.

I MAY HAVE BEEN LOST... **DAMAGED** WHEN WE MET, BUT **DON'T YOU DARE** LOOK AT ME AS SOME KIND OF PERPETUAL **VICTIM**.

I BOOKED THE FIRST FLIGHT BACK TO THE **UNITED STATES**...

I'M SORRY, GABRIELLE...

A FEW MONTHS LATER...

23

FOR MAYBE A FRACTION OF A SECOND, YOUNG **JEAN GREY** WAS ABLE TO DISTRACT HER FRIEND FROM DYING.

CHARLES XAVIER WASN'T THE ONLY BEING TO WITNESS THE BURGEONING PSYCHIC VIRTUOSITY OF THE LITTLE REDHEADED GIRL.

THE PHOENIX FORCE, A DEITY OF PURE ENERGY OLDER THAN THE UNIVERSE, WAS SEVERAL LIGHT-YEARS AWAY, SCOURING INFINITY FOR HER NEXT DIVINE, PHYSICAL HOST.

JEAN GREY CAUSED SUCH A BLIP IN THE COSMOS THAT THE PHOENIX COMPLETELY DIVERTED HER COURSE 180 DEGREES.

MANY INTERGALACTIC RACES HAVE SPENT LIFETIMES TRACKING THE PHOENIX FORCE, HOPING TO DOMINATE THE NEXT ENTITY WHO WILL PLAY HOST TO HER IMMEASURABLE GIFT.

THE SHI'AR EMPIRE ARE THE FIRST TO ACCURATELY MAP THE ABRUPT NEW TRAJECTORY OF THE MAJESTIC PHOENIX.

...A SMALL, PRIMITIVE PLANET CALLED EARTH.

SEND A RECONNAISSANCE VESSEL RIGHT AWAY!

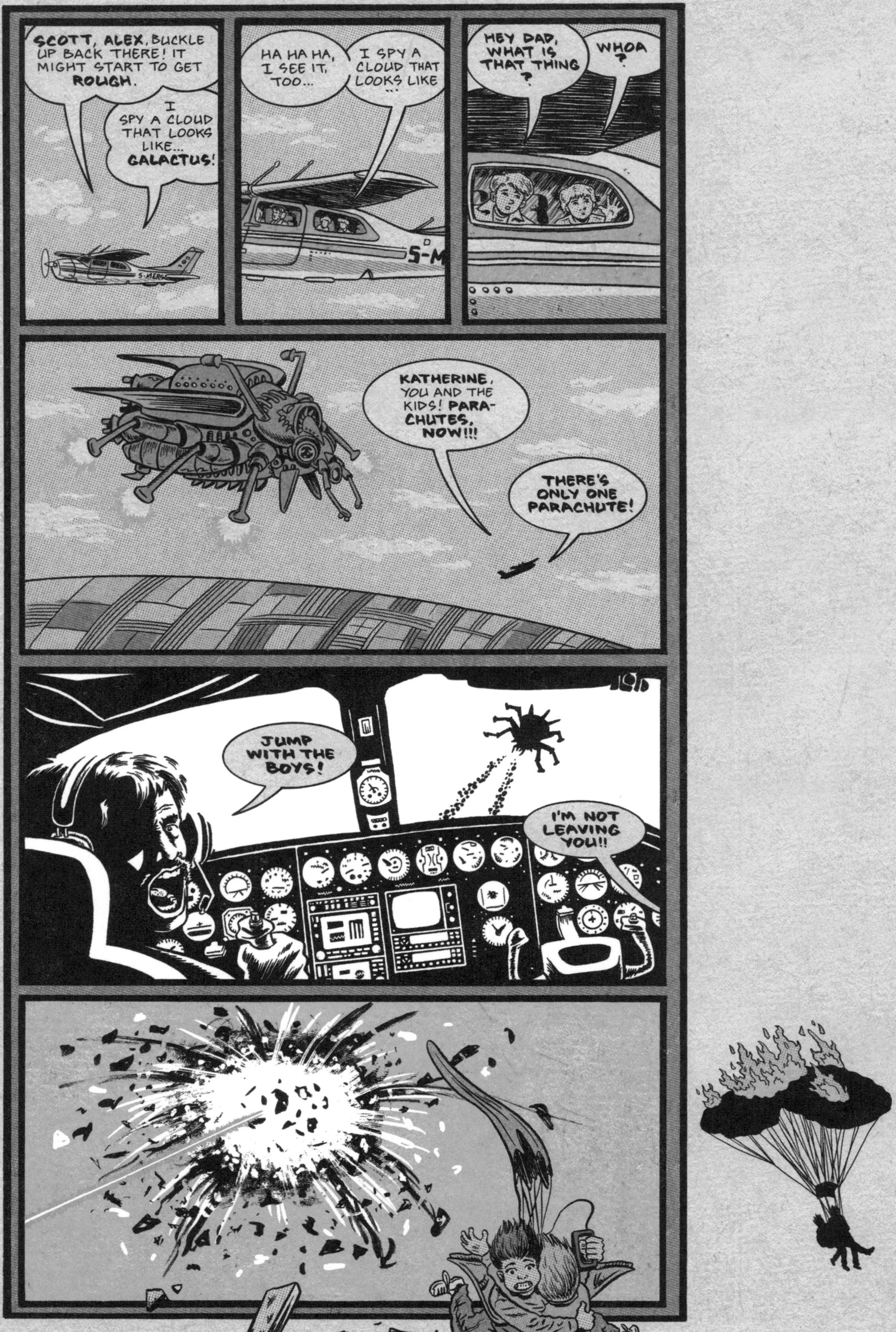

SCOTT, ALEX, BUCKLE UP BACK THERE! IT MIGHT START TO GET ROUGH.
I SPY A CLOUD THAT LOOKS LIKE... GALACTUS!
HA HA HA, I SEE IT, TOO...
I SPY A CLOUD THAT LOOKS LIKE ...
HEY DAD, WHAT IS THAT THING ?
WHOA ?
KATHERINE, YOU AND THE KIDS! PARA-CHUTES, NOW!!!
THERE'S ONLY ONE PARACHUTE!
JUMP WITH THE BOYS!
I'M NOT LEAVING YOU!!

THE PILOT, **CHRISTOPHER SUMMERS**, AND HIS WIFE WERE BEAMED ABOARD THE **SHI'AR** VESSEL AT PRECISELY THE MOMENT BEFORE THEIR CESSNA WAS **OBLITERATED.**

MY BOYS!

MONSTERS!

KATHERINE SUMMERS WOULD NEVER ALLOW HERSELF TO BE TAKEN EASILY...

CHRISTOPHER FOUGHT GALLANTLY AT FIRST. HE HAD **NOTHING** TO LOSE.

HE TOOK A FEW OF THEM DOWN BUT ONCE ALL ADRENALINE WORE OFF THE GUILT OF SURVIVING ERODED HIS SPIRIT COMPLETELY.

THE UNFORTUNATE THING ABOUT THE HUMAN INSTINCT FOR SELF-PRESERVATION IS THAT IT STILL EXISTS WHILE ON A PLANET-SIZED **PRISON COLONY.**

MOVE, GRUB'!!

YES...

SUMMERS RECALLS WALKING PAST THE BOUND MONSTER LONG ENOUGH TO REMEMBER WHEN THE CREATURE WAS **DOUBLE** ITS CURRENT SIZE.

GRUB!

QUIT STARING!

CHRISTOPHER GROWS TIRED OF HEARING THE BEAST WHIMPER.

C'MON, BUDDY. WE'RE GONNA HAVE COMPANY IN A MINUTE!

CH'OD, FRIEND?

BACK ON EARTH, THE **SUMMERS** BOYS' PARACHUTE ACTED LIKE A FLAMING BEACON FOR HELP BEFORE AND AFTER THEY SMASHED INTO THE REMOTE COUNTRYSIDE.

Scott...

Scott... are you okay?

ONCE THE STATE WAS SATISFIED THAT THE PARENTS WERE OUT OF THE PICTURE, **ALEX SUMMERS** WAS ADOPTED BY A NICE, ENCOURAGING COUPLE WHO PROMOTED ACADEMICS AND HARD WORK.

CAN WE GO VISIT MY BROTHER?

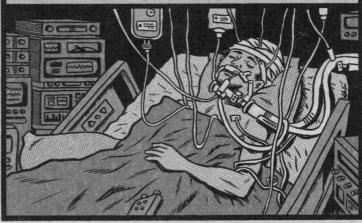

SCOTT SUMMERS WAS LESS FORTUNATE. THE DOCTORS COULDN'T TELL THE EXTENT OF POSSIBLE BRAIN DAMAGE WHILE THE BOY LAY COMATOSE.

HE WOKE UP A LITTLE MORE THAN A YEAR LATER...

HELP!

HELP ME!

EXCUSE ME, **JEAN**.

PLEASE DON'T BE FRIGHTENED. MY NAME IS **CHARLES**.

HUH ?

I'VE BEEN HERE FOR A LONG TIME. YOU'RE THE FIRST PERSON I'VE SEEN.

THAT'S WHY I'M HERE, **JEAN**. WHY DO YOU CHOOSE TO STAY ? ISN'T IT LONELY ?

MY FRIEND **ANNIE** WILL BE SCARED IF I'M NOT HERE WHEN SHE GETS BACK.

OH, CHILD. I'M SO SORRY. **ANNIE** ISN'T COMING BACK, I'M SAD TO SAY.

YOU'RE WRONG...

I KNOW I CAN BRING HER BACK IF I TRY HARD ENOUGH.

I WAS SENT BY YOUR **MOMMY** AND **DADDY** TO FIND YOU. THEY MISS YOU SO MUCH.

I MISS THEM, TOO. DO YOU THINK THEY'LL BE MAD AT ME FOR STAYING HERE SO LONG ?

NOT AT ALL. THEY'RE GOING TO BE THRILLED TO SEE YOU.

WHAT'S YOUR FAVORITE FOOD, **JEAN** ?

JEANNIE!

HOW CAN WE REPAY YOU, DOCTOR ?

MY BABY!

MAMA, I'M HUNGRY FOR PIZZA.

FOR YEARS, **SCOTT SUMMERS** COULDN'T REMEMBER ANYTHING FROM BEFORE HE WAS PULLED OUT OF RUBBLE AT THE HOSPITAL.

I HAVE A NOTE FROM THE DOCTOR TO WEAR THEM.

BUT YOU LOOK LIKE A DAMN GOOFUS, SLIM.

NO ONE SUSPECTED A **MUTANT** WAS BEHIND THE **DESTRUCTION**. THIS INFORMATION WOULD HAVE BEEN THE SPARK TO SET OFF A CIVIL WAR.

HEY!

LET ME TRY 'EM ON. IT'S ONLY FAIR...

NOW **SCOTT** IS THE OLDEST CHILD IN THE ORPHANAGE, NEARLY AGING OUT OF THE SYSTEM. HE DOESN'T RELATE WELL WITH THE YOUNGSTERS AT THE HOME.

I GET BAD HEADACHES WITHOUT MY GLASSES.

EW! YOU NEED 'EM MORE THAN ME, FOR SURE.

BEING AROUND KIDS HIS AGE DOESN'T PROVIDE MUCH COMFORT, EITHER.

QUIT LOOKIN' AT ME THAT WAY...

YER GROSSIN' ME OUT HERE...

...TAKE YER GLASSES...

AHHH!

WHA?

HUH?

TREVOR!

NO!

RUN!

NO, WAIT!

HELP!

HE'S A MUTIE!

HE'LL KILL US ALL!

≶ PANT ≶

...IT WASN'T...

≶ PANT ≶

...IT WASN'T MY FAULT...

30

"...THE FOURTH DAY THAT **BRIGHTON HEIGHTS** STUDENT **SCOTT SUMMERS** HAS INEXPLICABLY GONE MISSING. A CLASSMATE, **TREVOR DONOVAN** IS THE LAST KNOWN PERSON TO TALK WITH **SUMMERS**."

"HE JUST SPAZZED OUT, DROPPED HIS BOOKS AND RAN AWAY, KEPT SHOUTING 'I'M SORRY, I'M SORRY!' AND 'IT WASN'T MY FAULT, TREVOR! IT WASN'T MY FAULT!' WEIRD DUDE, HONESTLY."

MISSING

XAVIER COULDN'T BE SURE WHO PLANTED THE HALLUCINATIONS INTO **SUMMERS'** ALREADY FRAGILE MIND.

CHARLES WOULD NEED DIRECT ACCESS TO THE BOY TO UNCOVER THIS MYSTERY.

ONE THING IS CERTAIN, **SCOTT SUMMERS'** MUTANT ABILITIES ARE RAPIDLY DEVELOPING, AND IT COULD MEAN **DEVASTATION** IF HE FELL INTO CRIMINAL HANDS.

SSSEE, BOSSSS!

THIS IS BAD FOR US.

LOOKIT 'IM. HE'S A RIPE SQUARE. HIS MUM PROB'LY GOTTA WHOLE SEARCH PARTY ONNA HUNT FER 'IM AS WE SPEAK.

Hmmmm?

NO!

HA HA...

YOU WON'T TAKE ME AWAY!

WELL, YOUNG'UN, IT LOOKS LIKE WE GOTTA COUPLE THINGS IN COMMON...

WE'RE BOTH **MUTIES**, AN' WE'RE BOTH ONNA RUN

NAME'S **JACK O' DIAMONDS**

PUT 'ER THERE

SCOTT WAS LOOKING FOR HELP. FOR GUIDANCE. IT WAS EASY TO EXPLOIT THE CHILD'S INSECURITIES.

YOU SURE HE CAN HELP US?

KEEP MOVIN', KID...

BLAST RIGHT ABOUT THERE.

GOOD KID. GOOD KID.

I DON'T GET IT, **JACK**.

WHAT ABOUT MY **VISION** PROBLEMS?

PULL THAT LEVER, KID, AND DON'T STOP THE MACHINE UNTIL I SAY. **GOT IT?**

WITHIN SECONDS, **JACK O'DIAMONDS** CAN TELL SOMETHING IS INCREDIBLY WRONG.

SOME OUTSIDE FORCE PREVENTS HIM FROM VOCALIZING THE PROBLEM.

HE WAS AN EXTREMELY BAD MAN, **SCOTT.**

THE VERY CLOTHES YOU ARE WEARING WERE TAKEN FROM A BOY HE KILLED.

MY NAME IS **CHARLES XAVIER.** I FOLLOWED YOU HERE TO MAKE AN OFFER. I KNOW ABOUT YOUR MUTANT ABILITY AND I CAN TEACH YOU HOW TO CONTROL YOUR POWER.

LIKE **JACK,** IT SEEMS THERE ARE MANY MUTANTS IN THIS WORLD USING THEIR GIFTS FOR VERY **DESTRUCTIVE** PURPOSES.

THE TIME MAY COME WHERE WE MIGHT BE THE ONLY ONES WHO COULD STOP THEM.

MR. XAVIER, YOU CAN ADD ME TO THE LIST OF BAD MUTANTS. I'M A **MURDERER.** I--I KILLED A GUY...

ABOUT THAT...

CHARLES USES ALL OF HIS RESERVES, BUT CAN ONLY GET A FLASH OF **SCOTT SUMMERS'** PSYCHIC INVADER.

WHEN **CAPTAIN AMERICA** WAS ORIGINALLY UNLEASHED, THE **NAZIS** WERE UNDER TREMENDOUS PRESSURE TO GENERATE THEIR OWN **SUPER-SOLDIER**. THE RESULT WAS **WILHELM LOHMER**, A.K.A., **MASTER MAN**.

<...THE HELL?>

< HOW'D YOU GET DOWN HERE?>*

* TRANSLATED FROM GERMAN.

MASTER MAN BECAME A PROUD SYMBOL OF THE **THIRD REICH**, BARRELING THROUGH TOWN AFTER TOWN, DECIMATING MEN, WOMEN, AND CHILDREN, TO STAKE TERRITORY FOR THE NAZI **ÜBERMENSCH**.

< WHEN I WAS JUST A LITTLE BOY...>

<... I WATCHED YOU KILL MY MOTHER AND FATHER.>

IN THE DECADES FOLLOWING THE WAR, **MASTER MAN** HID IN **ARGENTINA** WITH A WHOLE GANG OF **AXIS WAR CRIMINALS**. HIS JOB WAS TO STAND GUARD OF ALL THEIR STOLEN LOOT AND PLUNDER.

IT WAS A CLOSELY GUARDED SECRET THAT THE SOURCE FOR ALL OF **MASTER MAN'S** POWER CAME FROM BIONICALLY ENGINEERING HALF HIS BODY WITH STATE-OF-THE-ART MACHINERY. RIGHT NOW, THE OTHER 50% IS IN COMPLETE AND TOTAL AGONY.

THIS COULD HAVE BEEN THE EIGHTH TIME IN HIS HIGH SCHOOL CAREER THAT **BOBBY DRAKE** IS SUSPENDED FOR GETTING BEAT UP.

THINGS ARE MORE SEVERE ON THIS OCCASION.

SOMEHOW, **DRAKE'S** BULLY CATCHES A SEVERE CASE OF **FROSTBITE** ON A BRIGHT JUNE DAY.

SHERIFF... I DON'T KNOW HOW YOUR SON GOT HURT! I'M BEING HONEST!!

STUFF IT, **BOBBY.**

YOU STILL GOTCHER SHOE-LACES, **BOBBY.** HANG YERSELF TONIGHT AND YOU'LL SAVE ME SOME TROUBLE IN THE MORNING.

34

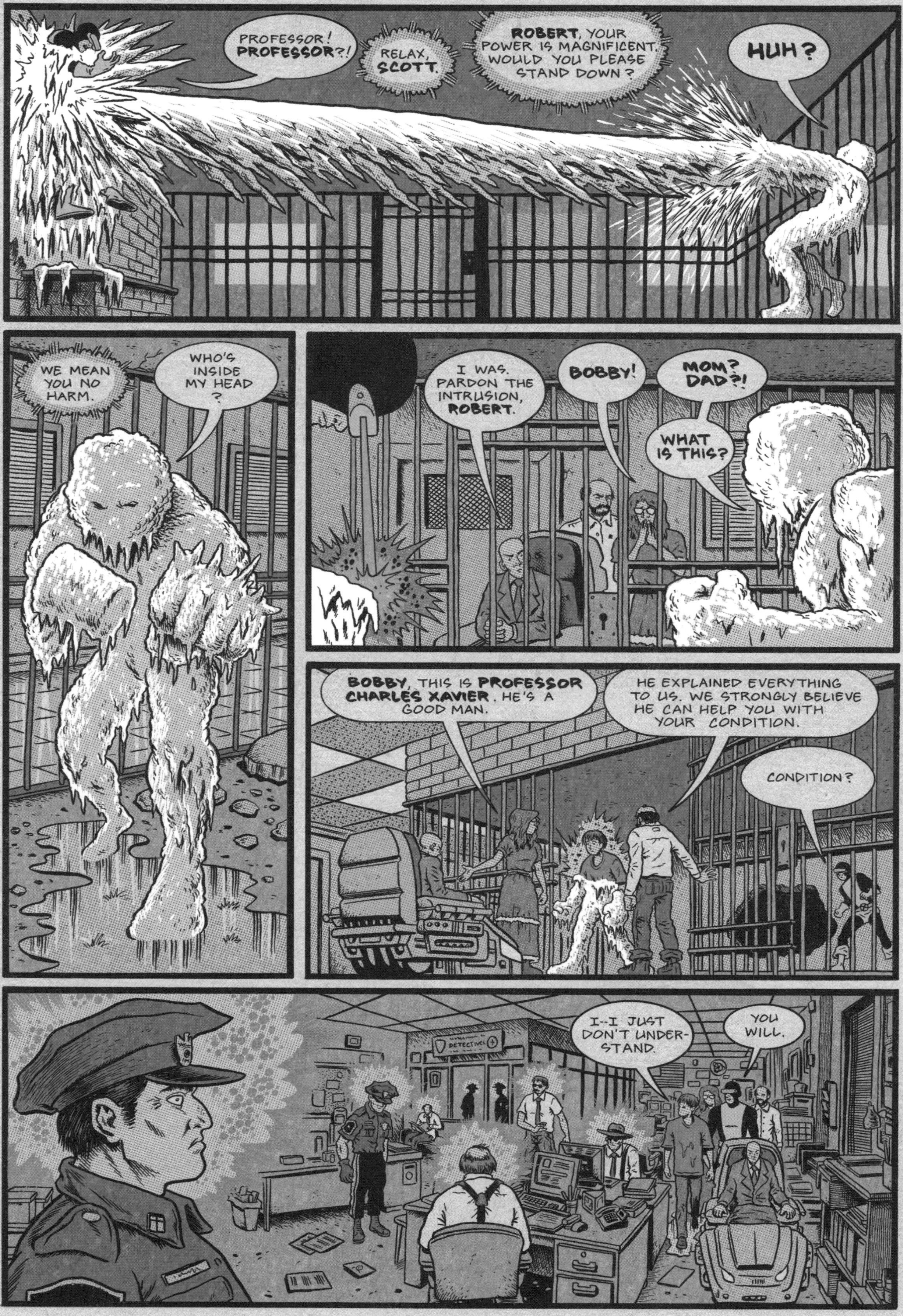
PROFESSOR! PROFESSOR?!
RELAX, SCOTT.
ROBERT, YOUR POWER IS MAGNIFICENT. WOULD YOU PLEASE STAND DOWN?
HUH?
WE MEAN YOU NO HARM.
WHO'S INSIDE MY HEAD ?
I WAS. PARDON THE INTRUSION, ROBERT.
BOBBY!
MOM? DAD?!
WHAT IS THIS?
BOBBY, THIS IS PROFESSOR CHARLES XAVIER. HE'S A GOOD MAN.
HE EXPLAINED EVERYTHING TO US. WE STRONGLY BELIEVE HE CAN HELP YOU WITH YOUR CONDITION.
CONDITION?
DETECTIVES
I--I JUST DON'T UNDER-STAND.
YOU WILL.

WANDA MAXIMOFF TRIED TO BE CAREFUL, BUT SHE GOT CAUGHT USING HER MUTANT POWERS, AND IN THIS CARPATHIAN VILLAGE, THAT IS A DEATH SENTENCE.

HER BROTHER IS DETERMINED NOT TO ALLOW THAT TO HAPPEN.

OH, NO!

I THINK...

...THEY SET...

...A TRAP...

PIETRO! WHAT DO WE DO NOW?

ARE... ARE THEY DEAD?

EVERY LAST ONE OF THEM...

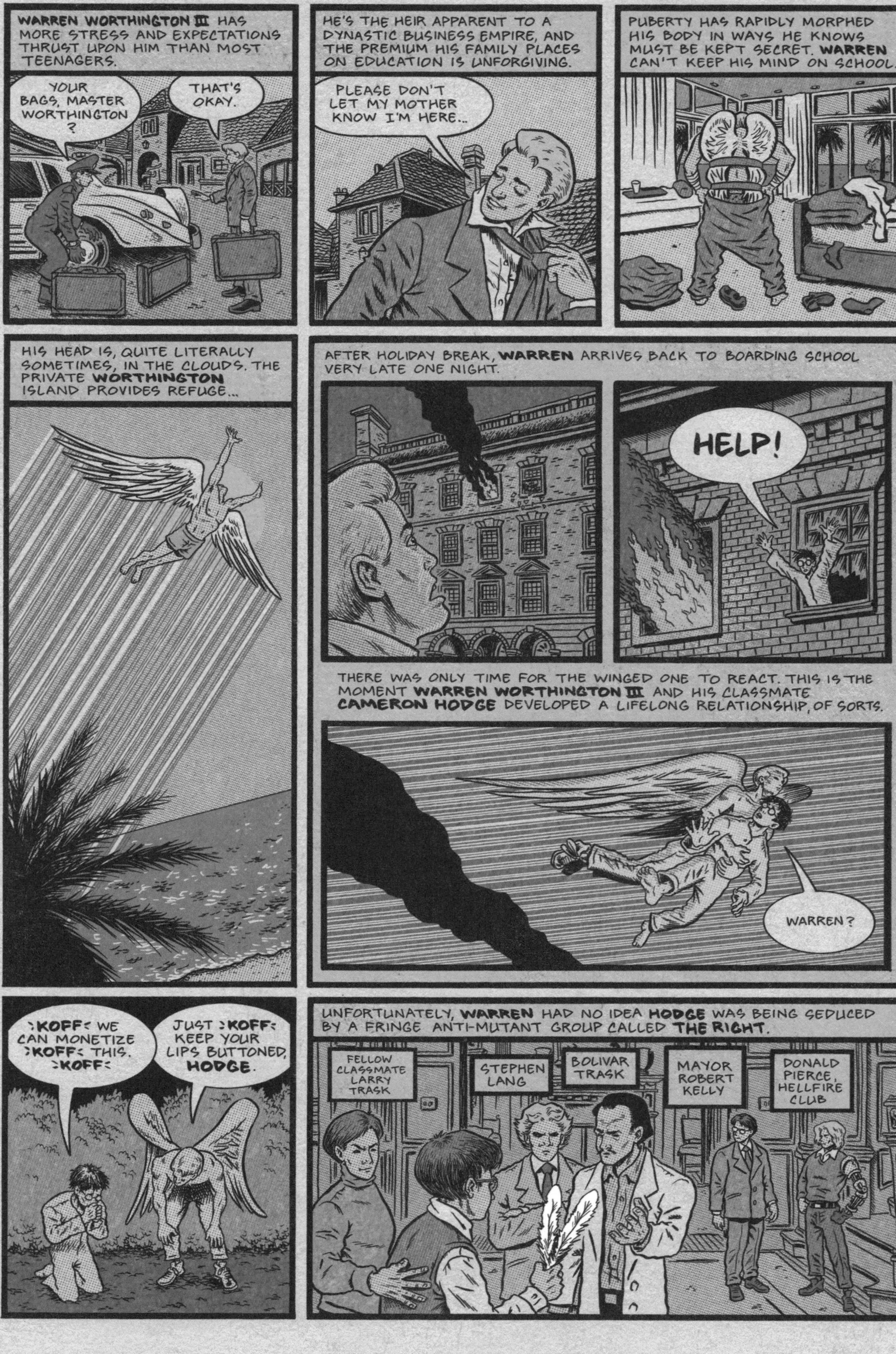
WARREN WORTHINGTON III HAS MORE STRESS AND EXPECTATIONS THRUST UPON HIM THAN MOST TEENAGERS.
YOUR BAGS, MASTER WORTHINGTON?
THAT'S OKAY.
HE'S THE HEIR APPARENT TO A DYNASTIC BUSINESS EMPIRE, AND THE PREMIUM HIS FAMILY PLACES ON EDUCATION IS UNFORGIVING.
PLEASE DON'T LET MY MOTHER KNOW I'M HERE...
PUBERTY HAS RAPIDLY MORPHED HIS BODY IN WAYS HE KNOWS MUST BE KEPT SECRET. WARREN CAN'T KEEP HIS MIND ON SCHOOL...
HIS HEAD IS, QUITE LITERALLY SOMETIMES, IN THE CLOUDS. THE PRIVATE WORTHINGTON ISLAND PROVIDES REFUGE...
AFTER HOLIDAY BREAK, WARREN ARRIVES BACK TO BOARDING SCHOOL VERY LATE ONE NIGHT.
HELP!
THERE WAS ONLY TIME FOR THE WINGED ONE TO REACT. THIS IS THE MOMENT WARREN WORTHINGTON III AND HIS CLASSMATE CAMERON HODGE DEVELOPED A LIFELONG RELATIONSHIP, OF SORTS.
WARREN?
:KOFF: WE CAN MONETIZE :KOFF: THIS. :KOFF:
JUST :KOFF: KEEP YOUR LIPS BUTTONED, HODGE.
UNFORTUNATELY, WARREN HAD NO IDEA HODGE WAS BEING SEDUCED BY A FRINGE ANTI-MUTANT GROUP CALLED THE RIGHT.
FELLOW CLASSMATE LARRY TRASK
STEPHEN LANG
BOLIVAR TRASK
MAYOR ROBERT KELLY
DONALD PIERCE, HELLFIRE CLUB

THERE WAS A DROUGHT FOR DECADES, BUT NOW THE HUMANS ARE EXPERIENCING A RESURGENCE OF SUPER-POWERED HEROES.

CAMERON HODGE INVESTS IN A PARTNERSHIP WITH WARREN WORTHINGTON, WHO JOINS THE BANDWAGON OF MASKED VIGILANTES.

LOOKS GREAT.

I'LL FIGHT THE CRIMES, YOU DO THE P.R.

HODGE ALSO PULLS HIS WEIGHT BY RAIDING HIS FATHER'S R&D FACILITY FOR WARREN'S SECRET WEAPON: KNOCKOUT GAS.

≋KOFF!≋

WHO IS THE AVENGING ANGEL

THE PICTURE NEWSPAPER

WARREN'S TREMENDOUS EGO PRE-DISPOSES HIM TO OVERLY ENJOY ALL THE PRAISE AND ADULATION.

CLAP CLAP CLAP CLAP CLAP

THEN IT'S DISCOVERED THAT THE KNOCKOUT GAS COMES WITH VERY HAZARDOUS SIDE EFFECTS.

"...WOULDN'T... WISH ≋GASP≋ THIS ON... ≋WHEEZE≋ MY WORST ENEMY... ≋HACK≋"

WARREN'S TREMENDOUS EGO NOW MAKES HIM SUSCEPTIBLE TO THE UNANIMOUS BACKLASH AND RECRIMINATION.

CAMERON...

...I QUIT...

PROFESSOR X KNOWS HE CAN BE MORE CONVINCING TO WARREN WHILE HE'S IN THIS VULNERABLE STATE.

?

HELLO, ANGEL. WE HAVE TO TALK...

AT CAMERON HODGE'S NEXT MEETING WITH THE RIGHT...

THE MUTANT AND I WON'T HAVE CONTACT LIKE BEFORE. HE'S TRANSFERRING TO SOME NEW SCHOOL OR SOMETHING.

SCOTTY, YOU'VE BEEN HERE THE LONGEST. WHERE DOES THE **PROFESSOR** DISAPPEAR TO ON WEDNESDAYS?

DON'T WORRY ABOUT IT...

HEY GUYS!

YOU GOTTA COME SEE THE NEWS! THE **BASTARD** DID IT!

SWISH!

SENATOR KELLY COULDN'T PASS A MUTANT REGISTRATION BILL, BUT HE DID SOMETHING WORSE...

"MY FELLOW **AMERICANS**, NOT A SOUL IN **NEW YORK CITY** WAS LEFT UNAFFECTED BY THE LIKES OF **NAMOR THE SUB-MARINER**..."

"...A ROGUE **MUTANT** WITH NO REGARD FOR HUMAN LIFE... NO RESPECT FOR THE VALUES OF THE **UNITED STATES**..."

"...WE WERE CAUGHT UNAWARE THOSE FEW DECADES AGO, AND WE'VE DONE LITTLE TO PREPARE FOR ANOTHER SUCH ATTACK..."

"...THAT IS, UNTIL NOW. HEAVEN FORBID ANY **MUTANT TERRORIST** THINKING IT CAN UPSET OUR FREEDOM AND WAY OF LIFE EVER AGAIN."

ARTIST INTERPRETATION

SENATOR KELLY SNUCK THROUGH A BILL PROVIDING FUNDING TO A SHELL COMPANY CONTROLLED BY **THE RIGHT**...

BOLIVAR TRASK NOW HAS THE MONEY TO CONDUCT TESTS ON THE SMALL AMOUNT OF MUTANT **DNA** HE KEPT ON ICE.

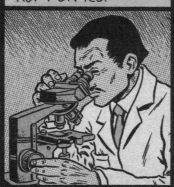

TRASK DISCOVERS THE GENETIC DIFFERENCE BETWEEN HUMANS AND MUTANTS, THUS CREATING A PATH FOR EFFECTIVE DETECTION.

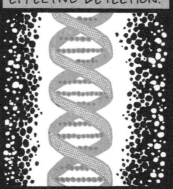

THE RIGHT'S GOALS ARE OFFENSIVE RATHER THAN DEFENSIVE.

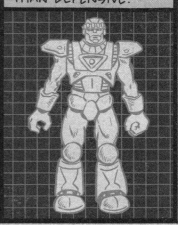

WEDNESDAY...

WE NEED TO ACCELERATE YOUR WORK. LIFT AND HOLD THAT CAR STEADY...

PROFESSOR, THAT'S TOO...

STOP TALKING!

COMMUNICATE WITH ME THIS WAY OR NOT AT ALL. NOW LIFT THE CAR!

STEADY. **STEADY**, I SAID!

HENRY McCOY'S BIGGEST CONCERN IS CHOOSING WHICH **IVY LEAGUE** UNIVERSITY WILL MOST COMPLEMENT HIS ACADEMIC PURSUITS.

$$X = \frac{-b \pm \sqrt{b^2 - 4c}}{2a}$$

HIS ATHLETICISM WILL ENSURE A **FULL SCHOLARSHIP** WHEREVER HE ENDS UP...

THEY HAVE **GUNS**!!

HAHA!

SUCKERS!!

?

HANK! STOP!

HENRY'S ACTIONS WERE RECORDED AND BECAME A VIRAL SENSATION ACROSS THE GLOBE.

THEY HAVE **RECORDERS** ON EARTH?

CHARLES XAVIER WAS ALREADY AWARE OF **McCOY** BEFORE THE TEENAGER'S GRANDSTANDING.

WHEN **XAVIER** AND HIS WARDS VISIT THE **McCOY** HOUSEHOLD TO TALK OF THEIR OWN BRAND OF ACADEMIC RECRUITMENT...

IT'S AS I FEARED...

YOUR UNIFORMS. **NOW!**

...McCOY, YOU'LL GET YOUR FREEDOM AFTER YOU HELP ME ACQUIRE SOMETHING I NEED FIRST.

WHAT MAKES YOU ENVISAGE I'D SUBSCRIBE TO SUCH A PROPOSAL?

SIMPLY PUT: YOUR PARENTS WILL ALSO DIE IF YOU AREN'T WILLING **AND** SUCCESSFUL.

WE'RE GIVING YOU 10 MINUTES, GENE-JOKE...

BE OUT IN FIVE.

MEET US 'ROUND BACK WHEN YOU GET IT!

GO!

ONE STEP CLOSER TO MY VERY OWN ATOMIC BOMB...

THANK YOU, HANK. HA HA.

I MUST CONFESS, THOUGH. I'M GONNA HAVE TO KILL YOU AND YOUR FAMILY ANYWAY. NO WITNESSES.

MASTER, MASTER. THE SNOW TASTES TASTY, YES?

SNOW? HUH??

HANK McCOY...

...WE HAVE YOUR FOLKS AT A SECURE LOCATION...

...SAFE AND SOUND!

PLEASE BEWARE OF THE CONQUISTADOR'S...

"...STUN BOLTS."

AAARGH!

SCOTT!

"FAILURE IS THE CONDIMENT THAT GIVES SUCCESS ITS FLAVOR." TRUMAN CAPOTE.

CRUSHING... CAN'T BREATHE...

MOVE AN INCH, ICE-BOY, AN' I SWEAR I'LL MELT YOU.

PROFESSOR... WE... NEED... HELP...

...DUUUH...DUH... DUUUUUUUH... DUH. ;GASP; DUUUUUH...DUH, DUH, DUH...DUH...

DUH...
DUUUH...

MASTER?

LITTLE TOAD?

TELL ME WHO DID THIS TO YOUR MASTER, LITTLE TOAD...

AFTER THE ORDEAL WITH **CONQUISTADOR**, IT ISN'T HARD FOR **HANK MCCOY** TO REALIZE WHERE HE BELONGS; ROUNDING OUT THE INAUGURAL CLASS OF THE **XAVIER SCHOOL FOR GIFTED YOUNGSTERS.**

LET ME TELL YOU THE STORY OF A MUTANT I MET NAMED **AMAHL FAROUK**...

THE YOUNG MUTANTS WILL NEVER FORGET THE HORRIFIC PORTRAIT **PROFESSOR X** PAINTS RECALLING THAT NIGHT IN **CAIRO** WHEN HE MOMENTARILY STEPPED INTO THE MIND OF A MAN PERVERTED BY HIS POWERS.

THE HOURS AT THE **XAVIER SCHOOL** ARE STRENUOUS. EIGHT HOURS OF SCHOLARSHIP IN THE CLASSROOM FOLLOWED BY EIGHT HOURS TRAINING EACH DAY IN THE **DANGER ROOM,** AN OBSTACLE-FILLED GYMNASIUM DESIGNED TO REFINE RAW MUTANT ABILITY INTO UNCANNY EXPERTISE.

OKAY, X-MEN. ON MY MARK.

YOU HEARD THAT LINE IN A MOVIE OR SOMETHING. DON'T LIE.

THE EARLIEST MISSIONS OF THE **X-MEN** ESTABLISHED THEIR OWN BRAND OF HUMANITARIAN AID.

HAPPY THANKS-GIVING!

WE BROUGHT PLENTY FOR EVERY FAMILY ON THE INSIDE.

WHAT IS THIS?

IT'S USING MAGIC TO BLOCK THE FLOOD.

WHY WOULD YOU TELL ME THIS? HOW COULD YOU DO IT?

MOIRA, YOU DIDN'T SEE THE GIRL'S **POWER.** SHE BOILED THE BRAINS OF A DOZEN MEN.

...UNTIL SHE MATURES... THOSE POWERS NEED TO BE MANAGED... RESTRAINED.

YOU'RE LOBOTOMIZ-ING HER, CHARLES! I DON'T LIKE IT!

MUIR ISLAND RESEARCH FACILITY...

DOCTOR MacTAGGERT...

...I HAD THE STRANGEST FEELING... MY DADDY WAS NEAR-BY. IS THIS POSSIBLE? AM I CRAZY? I'M NOT! AM I?

NO, **DAVID.** YOU KNOW EVERY-BODY ON THE ISLAND. NOW GO EATCHER BREAKFAST!

C'MON, **JAMIE!** SCRAMBLED EGGS!!

THE **X-MEN** ARE A FORTUNATE LOT. EXPOSED OR PHYSICALLY OBVIOUS MUTANTS FACE ALL DIFFERENT SORTS OF DISCRIMINATION, MAKING IT VIRTUALLY IMPOSSIBLE TO FIND EMPLOYMENT OR A PLACE TO LIVE.

YOU PAID YOUR NICKEL, LADIES 'N' GENTS! NOW FEAST YOUR EYES ON **THE BLOB**!

...A $100 PRIZE TO THE MAN WHO THINKS HE CAN LAY A SINGLE FINGER ON...

...UNUS, THE UNTOUCHABLE!

MANY MUTANTS NEED TO USE THEIR GIFTS SURREPTITIOUSLY TO ACQUIRE THE MOST BASIC THINGS NEEDED FOR SURVIVAL. A SUBSET OF THESE MUTANTS USE THEIR ABILITIES TO TAKE WHATEVER THEY WANT, WHENEVER THEY LIKE, WITHOUT A SECOND THOUGHT.

AN ADEQUATE PHOTO, **PARKER**. THE HEADLINE WILL READ... "**BROTHERHOOD OF EVIL MUTANTS** STRIKES AGAIN."

MR. JAMESON, I'LL NEED AN ADVANCE ON THAT. THE HELMET GUY SMASHED MY CAMERA WITH HIS MIND.

CHARLES XAVIER KNOWS THAT A CLASH IS INEVITABLE, BUT HIS **X-MEN** ARE NOWHERE NEAR BATTLE-READY.

CONCURRENTLY, THE UNQUENCHABLE **PHOENIX FORCE** CONTINUES THROUGH THE GALAXIES, ON HER WAY TO EARTH FOR THE ONE SOUL WORTHY OF HER POWER.

EPISODE 2

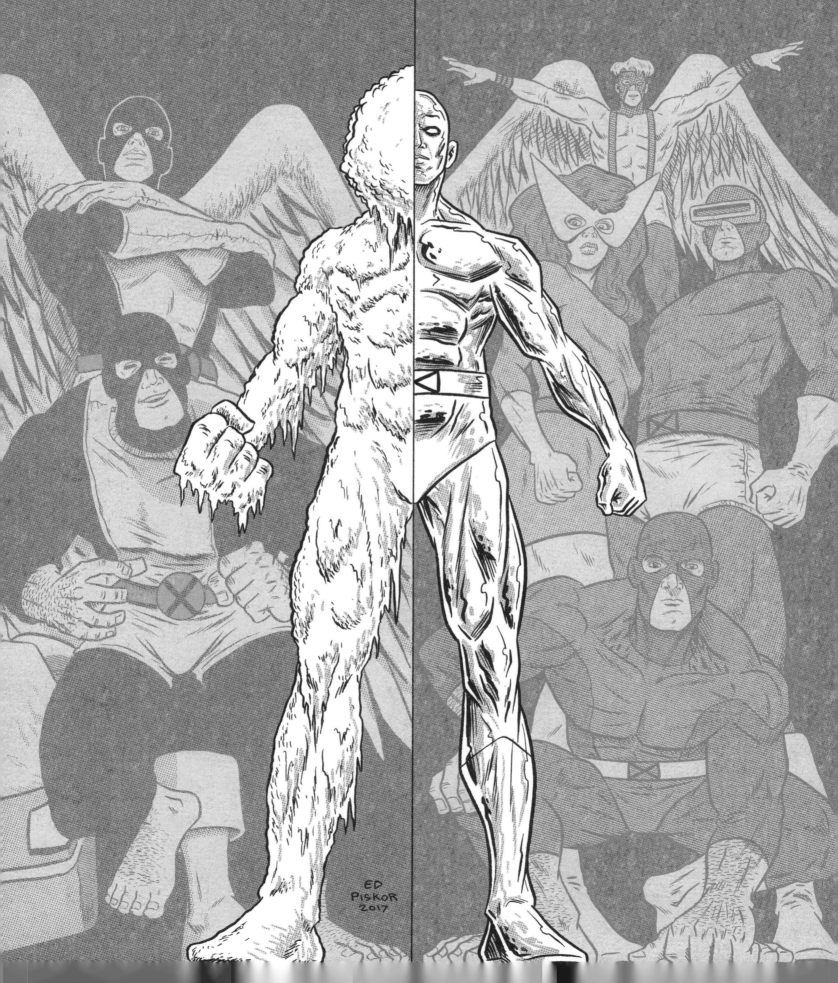

ED
PISKOR
2017

XAVIER AND THE X-MEN HAVE NO SUSPICIONS THAT A MARATHON OF EXTRATERRESTRIAL WARRIORS IS HEADING THEIR WAY...

...THE X-MEN AREN'T EVEN AWARE OF THE IMMINENT THREAT LOOMING JUST OUTSIDE OF THE EARTH'S ATMOSPHERE.

SANTO MARCO MAKES PERFECT STRATEGIC SENSE, MAGNETO...

WHAT'S THE PLAN?

SANTO MARCO, THE SELF-SUSTAINING ISLAND NATION JUST BARELY 50 MILES FROM THE COAST OF FLORIDA IS THE PERFECT PLACE FOR MAGNETO AND HIS BROTHERHOOD TO LAUNCH THEIR COLD WAR.

THE INHABITANTS OF THE ISLAND WAKE UP TO THE SOUNDS OF TWISTED METAL FORTIFYING THEM OFF FROM THE OUTSIDE WORLD.

MESMERO

BY NOON, MAGNETO'S TWO MASTERS OF HYPNOTISM AND ILLUSION COMPLETE THEIR PART OF THE PLOT.

MASTERMIND

BY DINNERTIME, MAGNETO IS KING AND THE REST OF THE WORLD IS NONE THE WISER.

OF COURSE THE MILITARY MIGHT OF THE U.S. IS MOST PROBLEMATIC...

...I'LL HAVE TO DO SOMETHING ABOUT THIS.

PERHAPS IN AN ACT OF HUBRIS AFTER CAPTURING **SANTO MARCO** SO EASILY, **MAGNETO** OVERPOWERS **CAPE CITADEL MISSILE BASE** IN FLORIDA BY HIMSELF.

XAVIER RUSHES THE **X-MEN** INTO BATTLE WITHOUT KNOWING EXACTLY WHAT **MAGNETO** IS PLANNING TO ACCOMPLISH.

WISELY, THE MASTER OF MAGNETISM DID SAVE A FEW TRADITIONAL MUNITIONS IN CASE HE MET AN OBSTACLE AND NEEDED A DIVERSION.

HE WAS EXPECTING THE **AVENGERS** AND IS VAGUELY INSULTED BY THE RESPONSE OF THIS NO-NAME BAND OF TEENAGERS.

WHERE'D THAT GUY GO?

JEAN? ARE YOU OKAY?

DID WE WIN, SLIM?

I DON'T KNOW...

THE **X-MEN** WEREN'T AFFORDED MUCH TIME TO CONTEMPLATE **MAGNETO'S** MOTIVES. DISENFRANCHISED MUTANTS ACROSS THE **U.S.** SWIFTLY BEGIN EXPRESSING THEIR ANGER WITH RECKLESS ABANDON.

ONE MUTANT'S RAMPAGE WAS SO SUCCESSFUL HE BYPASSED THE MOST POWERFUL DEFENSES PROTECTING **WASHINGTON, D.C.**

BOO!

THE **BLOB** AND THE **VANISHER** WOULD HAVE PULVERIZED THE **X-MEN** IF **CHARLES XAVIER** WEREN'T THERE ON BOTH OCCASIONS TO INTERVENE.

who am I??

who are you?

VILLAINS OF THIS CALIBER ARE NEVER INCARCERATED FOR LONG.

SO, WHAT'S THE CATCH?

YEAH, WHYD'JA BREAK ME OUTTA DA CLINK?

TELL ME ALL THAT YOU KNOW ABOUT THE MIGHTY **PHOENIX!**

THE WHO?

THE WHAT?

BOLIVAR TRASK'S PLAN COMES CLOSER TO FRUITION EVERY TIME A NEW MUTANT SHOWS AGGRESSION PUBLICLY.

MAGNETO'S MISSION AT THE FLORIDIAN MISSILE BASE WASN'T SIMPLY TO NEUTRALIZE THE NUCLEAR WEAPONS OF THE UNITED STATES...

HOW LONG HAS THIS GUY BEEN COOKING, **MAGNETO**?

I FEEL GOOD ABOUT THIS ONE, **MASTERMIND.**

...FOR HIS **GENETIC TRANSFORMATION CHAMBER** TO WORK HE NEEDS WEAPONS-GRADE **PLUTONIUM.**

YOU MAY STEP OUT NOW, MAYOR.

THE IDEA OF THE TECHNOLOGY IS TO EXPLOIT AND FORCE ANY MUTATED GENES IN REGULAR HUMANS TO MANIFEST PHYSIO-LOGICALLY.

HOW DO YOU FEEL?

I... UM...

MAGNETO WANTS 100% OF **SANTO MARCO'S** RESIDENTS TO BE CONVERTED AS MUTANTS WITHIN THE YEAR.

UH...UH... UH...UHH... UGH!

THE PROGRAM IS STILL IN ITS INFANCY, OF COURSE.

SIGH...

TOAD! COME CLEAN THIS MESS UP.

THIS MAD SCIENCE CAUSES **CEREBRO** TO GO HAYWIRE, THUSLY SHINING A SPOTLIGHT ON THE SECURELY REINFORCED AND SAFE-GUARDED ISLAND NATION.

GUYS!

BY THE TIME THE **X-MEN** PENE-TRATED **SANTO MARCO**, **MAGNETO** WAS NOWHERE TO BE FOUND. **XAVIER** STAYS BACK AT THE MANSION TO TRY AND PIN-POINT THE DESPOT'S LOCATION...

CLICK! CLICK!

THE BROTHERHOOD, HOWEVER, WAS THERE ON THE SHORES OF **SANTO MARCO** TO GREET THE **X-MEN**.

AH!

STOP!

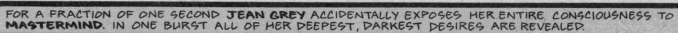

FOR A FRACTION OF ONE SECOND **JEAN GREY** ACCIDENTALLY EXPOSES HER ENTIRE CONSCIOUSNESS TO **MASTERMIND**. IN ONE BURST ALL OF HER DEEPEST, DARKEST DESIRES ARE REVEALED.

THE **X-MEN** CHALK UP THEIR FIRST OFFICIAL VICTORY.

SHOULD I CHASE THEM?

NO.

JEAN, WHAT HAPPENED THERE?

I... I NEED THE PROFESSOR.

THIS HOMELESS VAGRANT ALWAYS SHOWS UP WHEN **XAVIER** USES CEREBRO TO SCAN FOR MUTANTS.

LEMME HOLD TEN DOLLAHS, HOBO!

>HURM<

THE DERELICT SUFFERS FROM SEVERE AMNESIA THAT PREVENTS **CHARLES** FROM FINDING OUT VERY MUCH.

NO MONEY?

STOP!

A DIP IN THE **HUDSON RIVER** CHANGES EVERYTHING.

HA HAW!

THE FIRST THING ON **PRINCE NAMOR'S** REBOOTED MIND IS TO LET HIS KINGDOM KNOW HE'S ALIVE AND WELL.

NO!

NUCLEAR TESTING AND POLLUTION HAS DESTROYED **ATLANTIS. MAGNETO** KNOWS A THING OR TWO ABOUT SURVIVING GENOCIDE.

JOIN ME IN SWEET REVENGE, **NAMOR**...

THE **SUB-MARINER** DOESN'T NEED **MAGNETO'S** PERMISSION TO RAMPAGE THE AIR-BREATHERS.

NAMOR WAS IGNORANT OF THE NEW BREED OF SUPER HERO SEEKING TO TEMPER HIS CALAMITY.

COL. **FURY**, WHAT DO YOU SUGGEST?

I HATE TO SAY IT, BUT IT'S TIME TO UTILIZE **TRASK'S SENTINEL** PROGRAM.

COULD HE BE THE ONE **PHOENIX** IS SEARCHING FOR?

NOT POSSIBLE. THE **PHOENIX FORCE** WOULD NEVER BOND WITH AN AQUATIC CREATURE.

IT GOES WITHOUT SAYING THAT **MAGNETO'S** UNSUCCESSFUL IN TAMING **NAMOR** FOR HIS CAUSE, BUT THERE ARE MANY IMPRESSIONABLE MUTANTS LOOKING FOR A PLACE TO BELONG.

THE WINNER... AND STILL CHAMPION!

UNUS, THE UNTOUCHABLE!

MAGNETO DOESN'T WANT TO APPEAR DESPERATE. HOWEVER THE TRUTH IS HE NEEDS CONSIDERABLE HELP TO ACCOMPLISH HIS IMPERIALISTIC GOALS.

FASCINATING! YOU'RE NOT ONLY PHYSICALLY IMPOSSIBLE TO ATTACK...

...BUT, YOUR MIND IS ALSO RESISTANT TO PSYCHIC TRICKS.

THE INITIATION FOR **THE BROTHERHOOD** IS FRANKLY ARBITRARY, BUT **MAGNETO** WANTS **UNUS** TO BUILD AN INVESTMENT AND FEEL THAT HE'S EARNED HIS OPPORTUNITY.

YOU KNUCKLEHEADS THINK YOU'LL HAVE BETTER LUCK?

UNUS WAS A CAUTIOUS BEDFELLOW FOR **MAGNETO**, YET HE'S QUICKLY PROVING HIMSELF TO BE A FORMIDABLE ALLY.

BEFORE THE **X-MEN** COULD FORMULATE A PLAN FOR OVERCOMING AN IMPREGNABLE ADVERSARY...

BUSH-LEAGUE DORKS.

WHA?

THE **MUTANT MASTER** ALSO HAS CAUSE TO GENERATE SOME STRONG ALIGNMENTS FOR HIS OWN PURPOSES.

HOW DID YOU...?

UNUS, WHAT CAN YOU TELL ME ABOUT THE **PHOENIX**?

PHOENIX, PHOENIX, PHOENIX...

ONE OF **MUTANT MASTER'S** CHIEF LIEUTENANTS ON THE HUNT FOR THE **PHOENIX FORCE** IS **LUCIFER**, WHOSE MISSION RIGHT NOW IS TO PROCURE AS MUCH NUCLEAR MATERIAL AS HE CAN DISCOVER.

THIS AMOUNT OF **URANIUM** COULD ONLY LEAD TO THE CONCLUSION THAT A MASSIVE BOMB IS IN THE WORKS. THE **X-MEN** MAKE IT A PRIORITY TO DISCOVER THE CULPRIT.

ANGEL!

THEY ARE, TO SAY THE LEAST, VERY SLOPPY IN THEIR ATTEMPTS TO APPREHEND **LUCIFER**.

!!!

NO!

WHILE THE **X-MEN** SEARCH FOR **LUCIFER'S** BODY, THEY UNEARTH A GIANT WARHEAD LINKED TO HIS HEARTBEAT FOR DETONATION.

NOW THE GREEN WIRE, **SCOTT**... CAREFUL!

YES, PROFESSOR!

ANGEL, C'MON, WAKE UP, PAL! WAKE UP!!

OUT OF SIGHT FROM THE **X-MEN**, **LUCIFER** ADORNS HIS TRUE FORM, SLITHERS AWAY AND REPORTS VALUABLE INTELLIGENCE TO HIS LEADER.

HMMM... THERE WAS NO RADIO-ACTIVE SIGNATURE AROUND **LUCIFER'S** BOMB. WHY ELSE WOULD HE NEED THAT KIND OF **NUCLEAR** ENERGY?!

XAVIER SENSES A POSSIBLE CLUE SURROUNDING **LUCIFER'S** CRYPTIC PLANS...

CEREBRO IS ALERTING ME TO MUTANT ACTIVITY IN AN AREA I'VE NEVER EXPECTED.

ANTARCTICA...

NOT ARUBA... NOT TURKS AND CAICOS...

STRONG READINGS THROUGH THIS ROCK FOR SOME REASON.

THE **SAVAGE LAND** IS A SNAPSHOT OF **EARTH** FROM MILLIONS OF YEARS IN THE PAST WITH ONE MAJOR EXCEPTION: HUMANS ALSO INHABIT THIS AREA.

KA-ZAR AND THE **X-MEN** EVENTUALLY COME TO AN UNDERSTANDING.

>pant...<

>wheeze<

THE **X-MEN** COULDN'T FIND THE MUTANT THEY'VE BEEN TRACKING, BUT **KA-ZAR** SHOWS THEM WHERE THE MUTANT HAD RECENTLY BEEN.

POOR BASTARDS.

A COSMIC BEING TAKES NOTE THAT THE **MUTANT MASTER** MAY BE CLOSE TO DISCOVERING THE NEXT HOST FOR THE **PHOENIX FORCE** ON **EARTH**.

THE **STRANGER** STIRS THINGS UP TO TRY AND FLUSH OUT THE MOST POWERFUL CREATURES IN THE AREA.

WHAT IZZIS?

NO!

AN INVADER!

IT WORKS.

I'VE NEVER MET A BEAST WITH INHERENT POWER SUCH AS YOURS, YOU'LL COME WITH ME?

I WAS ABOUT TO ASK THE SAME THING, **STRANGER**.

MASTERMIND CAUGHT THE WORST OF THE WHOLE EXCHANGE...

HARD AS A ROCK...

THE **STRANGER** REGISTERED AS A MUTANT VIA **CEREBRO**, BUT THE **X-MEN** ARRIVED JUST AFTER THE ALIEN DISAPPEARED WITH **MAGNETO**.

HALFWAY TO **MARS** BY NOW.

I CAN'T EXPLAIN IT, BUT I CAN FEEL **MASTERMIND** IS STILL ALIVE IN THAT SHELL.

MAYBE THE **PROFESSOR** CAN HELP.

THIS IS DEFINITELY GOING TO BE A CHALLENGE.

EEEEEEEEEEEEEEEEE

HUH?

SOMEONE TRIPPED THE PERIMETER ALARM.

FIRST LINE OF DEFENSE: SLEEPING GAS

SECOND LINE OF DEFENSE: HOMING GRENADES

THIRD LINE OF DEFENSE: ELECTRIC FIELDS

LAST LINE OF DEFENSE: THE X-MEN!

THIS IS NOT A SIMULATION.

PREVENTED XAVIER'S PSYCHIC INTRUSION

CAIN MARKO?!

ULP!

HEY! MASTERMIND'S BODY IS MISSING.

THE MASS MEDIA'S PROPAGANDA SURROUNDING ESCALATED MUTANT HOSTILITY IS REACHING A TIPPING POINT.

MUTANT MENACE!

CHARLES XAVIER HOPED FOR INTELLECTUAL DISCOURSE DURING HIS TELEVISED DEBATE.

"MR. TRASK, IF YOU ARE PROPOSING TO HUNT DOWN MUTANTS LIKE DOGS...

"...THEN HOW COULD YOU POSSIBLY CALL OUTSPOKEN MUTANTS 'PARANOID'?"

UNFORTUNATELY, THE CONVERSATION COULD BE MORE ACCURATELY DESCRIBED AS A COMMERCIAL FOR BOLIVAR TRASK'S DEVIOUS GOALS.

THE SENTINELS EXCEL AT MUTANT DETECTION. THE UNFORSEEN ISSUE IS THAT THEY'LL DESTROY ANYTHING BETWEEN THEM AND THEIR TARGET.

THE SYNERGY OF THE X-MEN HAD TO BE FLAWLESS TO OVERCOME THE ROBOT PROTOTYPES AND EVEN STILL, THE MUTANT TEENAGERS ALMOST MET THEIR MATCH.

THE ONLY CASUALTY IN THE SCUFFLE IS THE CREATOR OF THESE DISCRIMINATORY WAR MACHINES.

BOLIVAR TRASK'S SON, LAWRENCE, KNOWS WHAT TO DO TO CARRY ON THE VISION OF THEIR SECRET CABAL, THE RIGHT.

I KNOW THE SECRET LOCATION OF THE MASTER MOLD.

WE CAN BEGIN PRODUCTION AGAIN SHORTLY.

60

ONCE THE EXCITEMENT OF BATTLE WORE OFF, **THE X-MEN** REALIZED THEY WERE DAMAGED FAR WORSE THAN THEY THOUGHT.

MY POOR STUDENTS. WHAT HAVE I BEEN PUTTING YOU THROUGH?

WHILE THE **X-MEN** ARE OUT OF COMMISSION, **MUTANT MASTER** TAKES THE OPPORTUNITY TO GENERATE AS MUCH FEAR, HATE AND DISTRUST AGAINST THEM AS POSSIBLE.

BANK

THE BLOB

UNUS "THE UNTOUCHABLE"

...WE ASSURE YOU...

...THE **X-MEN** WILL BE APPREHENDED ON SIGHT!

THE CONVALESCING MUTANTS ARE FORCED TO DISRUPT THEIR RECOVERY IN HOPES OF DISCOVERING THE SOURCE OF THE SMEAR CAMPAIGN.

THE TRAIL LEADS TO A WEAPONIZED SUPERCOMPUTER MORE POWERFUL THAN **CEREBRO**. THE MACHINE, **DOMINUS**, KNEW THE **X-MEN** WERE ON THEIR WAY AND HAD TIME TO PREPARE.

AFTER BEING DISMANTLED BY THE **X-MEN**, **BEAST** REALIZES THE COMPUTER WAS POWERED BY TREMENDOUS NUCLEAR ENERGY.

I BELIEVE **LUCIFER** WAS BEHIND THIS...

COUNT NEFARIA HAS BIG PLANS OF DOMINATION AND KNOWS THAT PATIENCE IS THE KEY TO SUCCESS.

YOU SAY A LIFE-SIZE HOLOGRAM IS POSSIBLE, TINKERER?

YESSIR.

HIS FIRST TASK IS TO CONTINUE DISCREDITING THE X-MEN.

A MUTIE!

RUN!

WHOA!

AAAH!

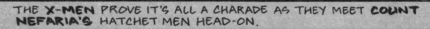

NEFARIA KEEPS THE RUSE GOING BY SIMULATING THE YOUNG MUTANTS' HOSTILE TAKEOVER OF THE CAPITOL BUILDING.

THE X-MEN PROVE IT'S ALL A CHARADE AS THEY MEET COUNT NEFARIA'S HATCHET MEN HEAD-ON.

THE DEFEAT OF NEFARIA'S LOWLY MERCENARIES IS A PYRRHIC VICTORY FOR XAVIER'S DISCIPLES...

HEROES OR VILLAINS?

THE VILLAIN'S TRUE MISSION WAS ACCOMPLISHED WHILE THE X-MEN HAD THEIR HANDS FULL.

YOU SAY THE DEVICE CAN ESCAPE ANY METAL DETECTION, TINKERER?

YESSIR.

NEFARIA KNOWS THIS TRUCK WILL BE HEADING TO NORAD EVENTUALLY...

GOOD. VERY GOOD.

IT'S TOO DANGEROUS FOR ME TO BE AN X-MAN. I... I THINK... I'M FINISHED.

TRY AS THEY MAY, THE **X-MEN** CAN'T CONVINCE **JEAN GREY** TO STAY WITH THE TEAM.

JEAN'S TRANSITION INTO A PURELY ACADEMIC LIFE WOULD ALWAYS BE TESTED AS NEW CATASTROPHES BEFALL THE CITY OF **NEW YORK**.

SHE WOULD DROWN HERSELF IN HER STUDIES AS A DISTRACTION.

...THE RENAISSANCE FAIR IS THIS WEEKEND.

HUH?

I HAVE TO GET BACK. THIS WAS FUN, THOUGH, **MORDECAI**.

...UM, ARE YOU SURE? UHH... OKAY...

WHEN **JEAN** WAS ABLE TO PUSH HER AFFECTIONS FOR **SCOTT SUMMERS** TO THE BACK OF HER MIND, HER ROMANTIC INTERESTS BECAME ENTERTAINED BY **TED ROBERTS**, A STAR ATHLETE AT **METRO UNIVERSITY**.

HMRPH!

I CONFESS MY FIRST ATTEMPT WAS A **FAILURE**, BUT I'M LEARNING MORE AND MORE ABOUT HER...

WE'LL GET HER...

I PROMISE SHE'LL BE OURS!

63

CALVIN RANKIN HAS THE UNIQUE ABILITY TO MIMIC THE ATTRIBUTES OF FELLOW MUTANTS WITHIN A CLOSE PROXIMITY.

DOES THAT RED-HEAD GIRL THINK IT'S CREEPY YOU'RE IN EVERY CLASS SHE TAKES?

I DON'T GIVE A CRAP.

HE'S NEVER HAD THE CHANCE TO EXPLOIT SUCH A POWERFUL MUTANT AS JEAN GREY.

GREAT JOB ONCE AGAIN, RANKIN.

ACADEMICS IS, LIKE, IMPORTANT STUFF, PROF.

ONE DRAWBACK TO RANKIN'S POWER IS THAT HE DOESN'T NECESSARILY KNOW WHEN HE'S NEAR A MUTANT UNTIL IT'S TRIGGERED INVOLUNTARILY.

JEANNIE! LONG TIME NO SEE!

WHERE'S SCOTT?

A STINKIN' GENE-JOKE!

TAG 'IM AN' BAG 'IM!!

STOP PUMMELLING THOSE KIDS.

OR WHAT?

CALVIN RANKIN, YOU HAVE PROVED YOUR POINT.

STEP OUT OF MY WAY, CUE-BALL...

I'LL BE HAPPY TO MOVE ASIDE, BUT FIRST, A QUERY...

... HAVE YOU EVER HEARD OF THE X-MEN?

JEAN GREY'S ABSENCE FROM THE X-MEN ISN'T LOST ON OPPORTUNISTIC VILLAINS. THE **BANSHEE** IS THE NEXT PAWN USED IN AN EFFORT TO FURTHER DWINDLE THE TEAM'S NUMBERS.

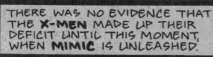
THERE WAS NO EVIDENCE THAT THE **X-MEN** MADE UP THEIR DEFICIT UNTIL THIS MOMENT, WHEN **MIMIC** IS UNLEASHED.

BANSHEE COMES TO HIS SENSES WHEN THE MIND CONTROL DEVICE IS DESTROYED.

MIMIC DOESN'T NOTICE...

STOP IT!

MIMIC, WHAT IS WRONG WITH YOU?

BANSHEE REVEALS HE WAS A MERE BRAINWASHED TOOL IN A MUCH BIGGER CONSPIRACY.

...HE'S OBSESSED WITH AN ALIEN CALLED **PHOENIX**...

MIMIC, YOU WERE NOT AUTHORIZED TO ENGAGE IN BATTLE... YOUR VICIOUS BEATING OF **BANSHEE** IS UNFORGIVABLE... YOUR...

I GET THE PITCHER. SEE YA 'ROUND.

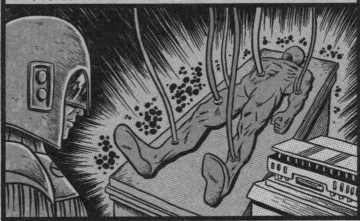

INSPIRED TO FIGHT FIRE WITH FIRE, **MUTANT MASTER** USES UNSTABLE MOLECULES TO DESIGN A **MIMIC** OF HIS VERY OWN.

SUPER-ADAPTOID'S TRIAL RUN AGAINST THE **AVENGERS** WAS A MODERATE SUCCESS AND HELPED SHAPE ITS AESTHETIC.

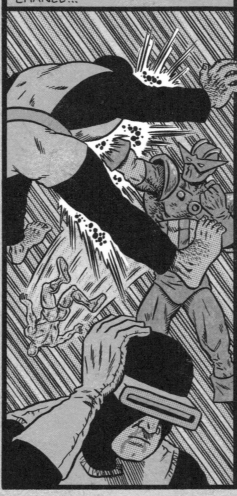

WHEN THE CREATURE MET THE **X-MEN**, THEY DIDN'T STAND A CHANCE...

...UNTIL...

...A DANGEROUS BIOFEEDBACK LOOP ENGULFS BOTH THE **SUPER-ADAPTOID** AND **MIMIC** AS THEY TRY TO ABSORB EACH OTHER'S POWERS.

THE RESULTING EFFECTS DE-STROY THE **ADAPTOID** AND RENDER **MIMIC'S** MUTANT ABILITY COMPLETELY IMPOTENT.

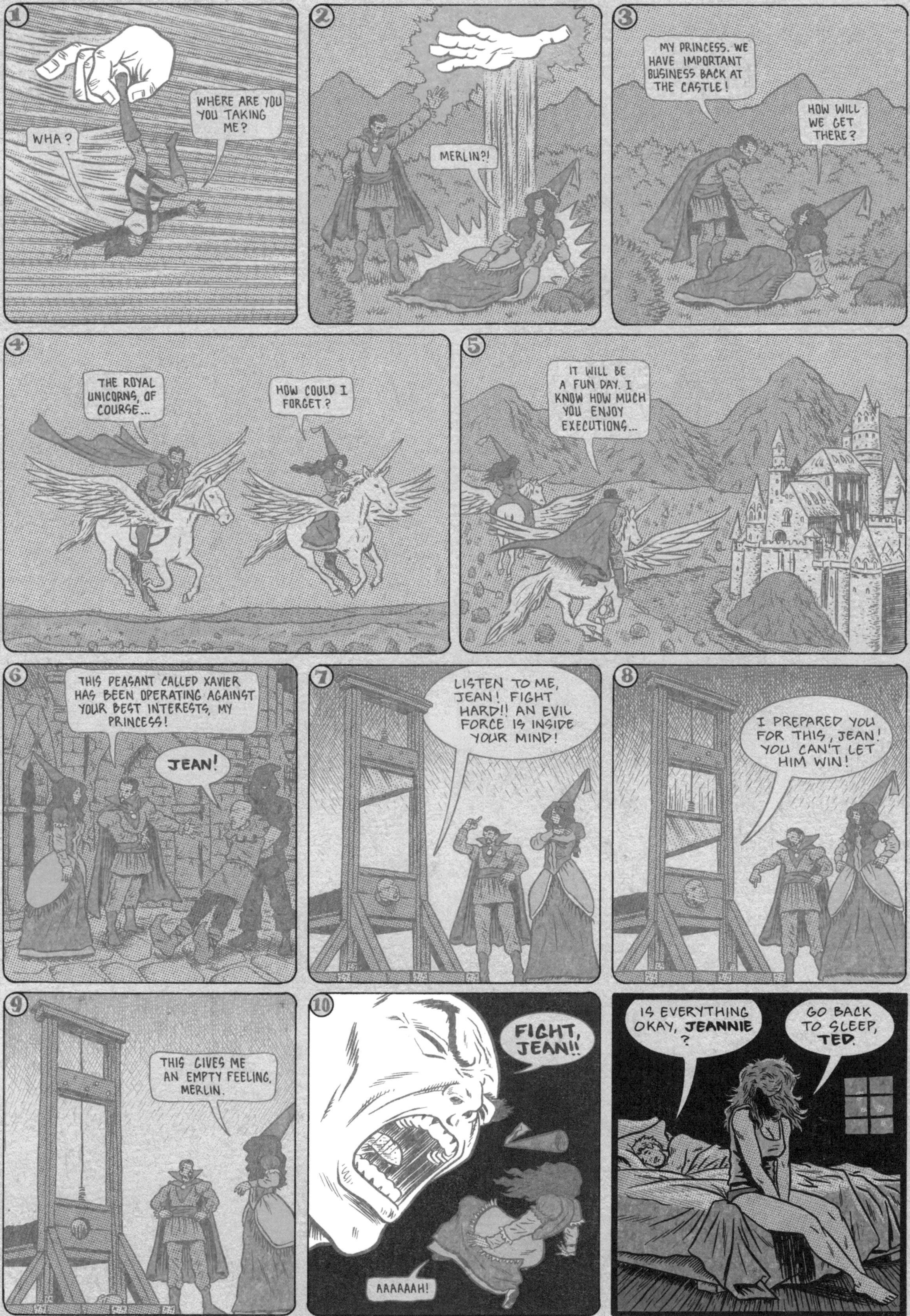
WHA?
WHERE ARE YOU YOU TAKING ME?
MERLIN?!
MY PRINCESS. WE HAVE IMPORTANT BUSINESS BACK AT THE CASTLE!
HOW WILL WE GET THERE?
THE ROYAL UNICORNS, OF COURSE...
HOW COULD I FORGET?
IT WILL BE A FUN DAY. I KNOW HOW MUCH YOU ENJOY EXECUTIONS...
THIS PEASANT CALLED XAVIER HAS BEEN OPERATING AGAINST YOUR BEST INTERESTS, MY PRINCESS!
JEAN!
LISTEN TO ME, JEAN! FIGHT HARD!! AN EVIL FORCE IS INSIDE YOUR MIND!
I PREPARED YOU FOR THIS, JEAN! YOU CAN'T LET HIM WIN!
THIS GIVES ME AN EMPTY FEELING, MERLIN.
FIGHT, JEAN!!
AAAAAAH!
IS EVERYTHING OKAY, JEANNIE?
GO BACK TO SLEEP, TED.

IT WOULD BE A DRASTIC UNDERSTATEMENT TO SUGGEST THAT **JEAN GREY** ESCAPED THE SUPER-HERO LIFESTYLE WHILE AT **METRO UNIVERSITY.**

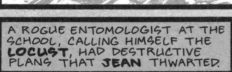

A ROGUE ENTOMOLOGIST AT THE SCHOOL, CALLING HIMSELF THE **LOCUST**, HAD DESTRUCTIVE PLANS THAT **JEAN** THWARTED.

SHE SOLICITED THE HELP OF THE **X-MEN** WHEN **KUKULKAN** RAIDED THE ARCHAEOLOGY DEPARTMENT FOR A RECENTLY UNEARTHED, ANCIENT MAYAN PENDANT.

THE **DAILY BUGLE** CALLED THIS WALKING ATOMIC BOMB **COBALT MAN.** THE **X-MEN** MADE SHORT WORK OF HIM, BUT THE PUBLIC DIDN'T HATE THEM ANY LESS.

ALL OF THIS MANIA LED TO ONE FOREGONE CONCLUSION...

WELCOME BACK, JEANNIE!

YOU WERE MISSED!

FOCUS, PEOPLE!

HA.

DON'T FRONT, **SCOTT.**

CHARLES XAVIER FEELS A FRATERNAL RESPONSIBILITY TO HELP CAIN MARKO OUT OF HIS CATATONIA EVEN AFTER ALL THE DEVASTATION CAUSED IN HIS WAKE.

AS MUCH AS I DISLIKE IT, I MUST INTRUDE UPON YOUR PSYCHE ONCE AGAIN.

THIS HAS NEVER HAPPENED BEFORE, CAIN!

WHAT ARE YOU TRYING TO TELL ME?

CAIN?

IT'S HERE...

X-MEN!

I CAN FEEL IT!

69

WHERE... ...WHERE'S THE PROFESSOR?

JUGGERNAUT KNOWS THAT THERE IS ONLY ONE THING THAT CAN BE CALLING TO HIM WITH SUCH POWERFUL ENERGY: THE CRIMSON GEM OF CYTTORAK.

HOWEVER, HE WASN'T EXPECTING BANSHEE'S EVIL COUSIN, BLACK TOM CASSIDY, TO HAVE HIS FOUL HANDS CLUTCHING THE PRIZED CRYSTAL.

GIMME MY RUBY!!

AY, BOYO, LOOKS LIKE YE HAVE FAMILY TROUBLES, TOO, EH?

PROFESSOR XAVIER?

PROFESSOR?

PROFESSOR ????

NO LUCK, JEAN?

DR. DOOM, MOLE MAN... NONE OF OUR BIGGEST SUSPECTS HAVE ANY SOLID INFORMATION ON XAVIER'S WHEREABOUTS...

...SERVES THE LITTLE MUTIE SYMPATHIZER RIGHT...

...SOMETHING IS BREWING IN SCOTLAND, BUT IT'S OUT OF OUR JURISDICTION.

INSPIRED BY THIS POSSIBLE LEAD REGARDING PROFESSOR X'S LOCATION, JEAN GREY ATTEMPTS TO BOOST HER EXISTING MENTAL POWERS IN A WAY SHE'S NEVER TRIED BEFORE...

COINCIDENTALLY, BANSHEE HAS BEEN TRACKING MUTANT MASTER ACROSS EUROPE.

ARE YOU POSITIVE, BANSHEE?

YES, JEAN. THEY HAVE XAVIER!

I'M ON MY WAY TO GO GET 'IM FER YE...

...LEAST I C'N DO...

BANSHEE, LOOK OUT!

BANSHEE!

CAN WE JUST **KILL** THE RED-HEAD THIS TIME?

NO! THE MIND-CONTROL TECHNOLOGY I'LL NEED FOR **XAVIER** IS FAR MORE POWERFUL THAN EARLIER VERSIONS. THE **BANSHEE** WILL BE OUR TEST SUBJECT.

MUTANT MASTER HAS BEEN ON **EARTH** LONG ENOUGH TO MAKE A DETERMINATION, WITHIN A HIGH PROBABILITY, THAT **CHARLES XAVIER** WILL BE THE INEVITABLE HOST OF THE ENCROACHING **PHOENIX FORCE**...

...IF WE ARE ABLE TO TAKE OVER HIS EVERY THOUGHT BEFORE THE DAY HE MAKES CONTACT...

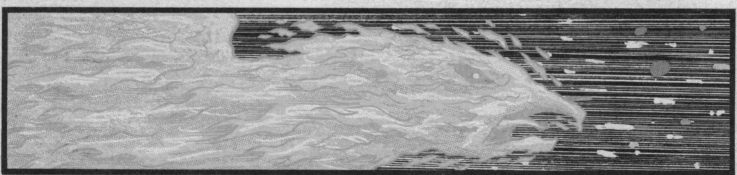

"...WE WILL MAKE THE **PHOENIX** OUR PUPPET AND WIELD ULTIMATE POWER IN EVERY KNOWN UNIVERSE."

I CAN HAVE NO DISRUPTIONS WHEN I BEGIN TO BRAIN-WASH **XAVIER**.

THE **X-MEN** ARE SURELY ON THEIR WAY. DESTROY THEM!

THIS MUTANT CALLED **FORGE** WAS COMMISSIONED BY **XAVIER** TO BUILD MOST OF THE X-MEN'S TECHNOLOGY.

THE **DANGER ROOM** AND THE **BLACKBIRD** JET ARE SOME OF HIS MOST AMBITIOUS CREATIONS.

THE **BLACKBIRD** IS COMPLETELY INVISIBLE TO EVERY EARTHLY FORM OF RADAR.

FORGE DIDN'T ACCOUNT FOR AN EXTRATERRESTRIAL ADVERSARY.

THE **X-MEN'S** TRAINING DID, HOWEVER, COVER CONTINGENCIES SUCH AS THIS.

THE KIDS STILL HAVE A LOT TO LEARN.

CYCLOPS' LAST CONSCIOUS THOUGHT IS THAT, BY BEING ATTACKED, THEY MUST BE IN THE CORRECT PLACE.

WHEN HE WAKES UP HIS SUSPICIONS ARE CONFIRMED.

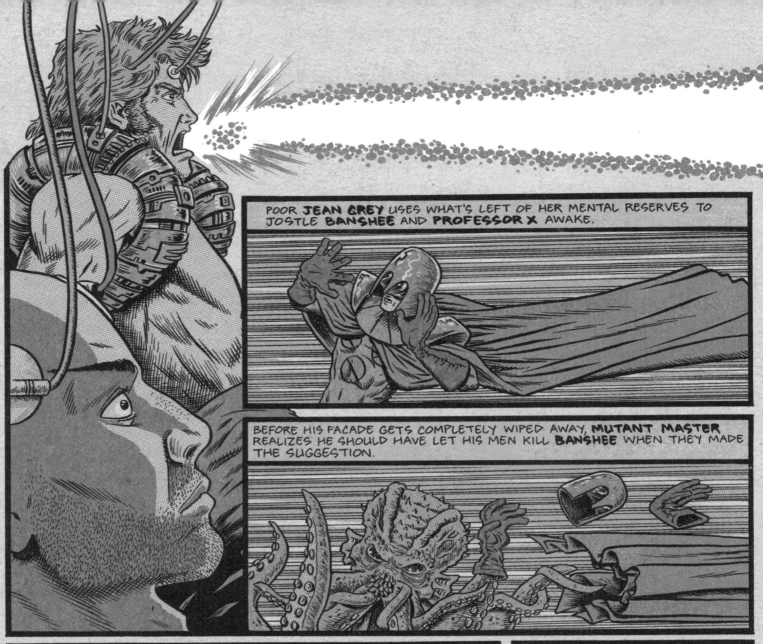

POOR **JEAN GREY** USES WHAT'S LEFT OF HER MENTAL RESERVES TO JOSTLE **BANSHEE** AND **PROFESSOR X** AWAKE.

BEFORE HIS FACADE GETS COMPLETELY WIPED AWAY, **MUTANT MASTER** REALIZES HE SHOULD HAVE LET HIS MEN KILL **BANSHEE** WHEN THEY MADE THE SUGGESTION.

NOW THAT **MUTANT MASTER** IS EXPOSED, HE CHOOSES THE ONLY ACCEPTABLE OPTION FOR A DISGRACED MEMBER OF HIS SPECIES...

GIT THAT LYING SUCKER!

...SELF-DESTRUCTION!

RUN...

...RUN!

 **MUTANT MASTER'S** DEMISE HAS TRIGGERED A MASSIVE ALIEN HORDE HEADING TO **EARTH** SPECIFICALLY FOR ME...

 **XAVIER** TELLS HIS PUPILS WHAT HE LEARNED OF THE **PHOENIX** WHEN HE WAS HELD CAPTIVE.

 **CHARLES** ATTEMPTS TO CAST INFLUENCE OVER THE ARTIFICIAL MIND OF THE **CHANGELING** ANDROID.

 HE MUST DEVOTE ALL OF HIS INTELLECT TO DEFENDING AGAINST THE INVASION WITHOUT DROPPING OUT OF SIGHT.

CEREBRO DISCOVERED THAT A MURDEROUS MUTANT USES SUBTERRANEAN **MANHATTAN** TO HIDE OUT.

GROTESK KILLED DOZENS BEFORE THE **X-MEN** PINPOINTED HIS LOCATION.

ONE MORE BODY GETS ADDED TO THE LIST WHEN THEY ARRIVE.

NO!!

 THE **X-MEN** NOW THINK THIS WAS **PROFESSOR X'S** PLAN THE ENTIRE TIME.

THE **X-MEN** WERE INCREDIBLY UNCOMFORTABLE KEEPING UP THE DECEP-TION TO THE EXTENT **XAVIER** REQUIRED, BUT THEY HAD TO TRUST THE RUSE WAS FOR A GREATER PURPOSE.

...DUST TO DUST...

>SOB...<

AFTER WHAT SEEMED LIKE AN ETERNITY, **MAGNETO** WAS BACK ON PLANET **EARTH**, FAR FROM THE **STRANGER'S** DOMINION.

THE **STRANGER** COLLECTED BEINGS HE THOUGHT MIGHT BE POTENTIAL SUITORS FOR THE ALL-POWERFUL **PHOENIX FORCE**.

<YOU'LL HAVE SOME COMPANY UNTIL I PREPARE AN EXHIBIT FOR THIS NEW ONE.>*

* TRANSLATED FROM ALIEN LANGUAGE. -- ED

IT WAS AN ACT OF FOLLY TO PUT A METAL MACHINE MAN NEAR **MAGNUS**.

THE MASTER OF MAGNETISM LOCATES A VESSEL OF FAMILIAR ALLOYS. HE DOESN'T NEED TO BE A MASTER PILOT TO ESCAPE.

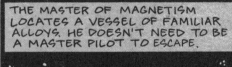

THIS CAN, HOWEVER, MAKE FOR A VERY HARSH LANDING.

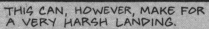

MAGNETO SWORE WHEN HE TOUCHED DOWN HE WAS SOMEWHERE IN **ANTARC-TICA**, BUT AFTER EMERGING FROM THE RUBBLE HE REALIZES HE'S IN PARADISE.

NOW, HERE HE STANDS...

GOODBYE, **CHARLES**...

SILLY FOR THE **X-MEN** TO THINK THEY COULD FIND REFUGE FROM THEIR DECEPTION BACK AT THEIR MANSION.

YOU MUTIES HAVE FIVE MINUTES TO CLUE ME IN ON WHAT'S GOIN' ON.

WE KNOW THAT **XAVIER** AIN'T DEAD.

MY GUYS ARE TRACKING HIM ACROSS THE COUNTRY AS WE SPEAK. WE GOT WAYS UH SEEIN' THROUGH HIS DISGUISES.

SO TELL ME. WHAT'S WITH ALL THE SHENANIGANS?

THE TOTAL INSUBORDINATION OF **XAVIER'S** YOUNG STUDENTS PUSHES THE HAND OF **NICK FURY**, AGENT OF S.H.I.E.L.D. *

...EFFECTIVE IMMEDIATELY, THE **X-MEN** TEAM ARE NO LONGER TO OPERATE UNLESS DIRECTLY AUTHORIZED BY **ME**...

...DISOBEDIENCE WILL BE CONSIDERED AN ACT OF **TERRORISM**.

* STRATEGIC HAZARD INTERVENTION ESPIONAGE LOGISTICS DIRECTORATE

FURY SAID NOTHING ABOUT PREVENTING THE BAND OF MUTANTS FROM OPERATING INDEPENDENTLY WHILE CARRYING ON **PROFESSOR X'S** MISSION.

 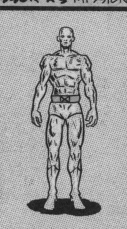   

OFF THE SHORES OF **LONG ISLAND**, THE **ANGEL** MEETS A MYSTERIOUS **RED RAVEN**.

WITHIN EYESHOT OF THEIR SCUFFLE, A YOUNG MUTANT NAMED **JOHN** FALLS INTO AN ABRUPT TRANCE...

HOME...

IN **SAN FRANCISCO**, **BEAST** AND **ICEMAN** REALIZE THEIR DEFICIENCIES OUTSIDE OF THE TEAM DYNAMIC.

IN **MISSISSIPPI**, **ANNA MARIE** LEAVES HOME. SHE, TOO, IS A PUPPET UNDER A SPELL.

SAVAGE...

...LAND...

CYCLOPS AND **MARVEL GIRL** WERE JUST SUPPOSED TO BE ON VACATION.

IN THE **FLORIDA** PANHANDLE, THE FIRST LOT OF DAZED, SEDUCED MUTANTS BEGIN SHOWING UP TO BE WHISKED AWAY.

LORNA DANE'S MIND KEEPS SWIMMING WITH VISIONS OF THE **SAVAGE LAND**... OF FAMILY.

HOME...

WATCH OUT!

BOBBY DRAKE'S REFLEXES REMAIN SHARP...

YOU OKAY, GIRL?

...BUT PERHAPS **ICEMAN'S** INSTINCTS AREN'T SHARP ENOUGH...

WHOA!

LIKE A SUPERNOVA, **LORNA DANE** BURNT HERSELF OUT STRAIGHTAWAY.

HANK! WE GOTTA HELP THIS GIRL! SHE'S A MUTANT ON THE FRITZ!

GOODNESS!

WEIGHING THEIR OPTIONS, **HENRY McCOY** SEEKS A SECOND OPINION.

SHE MAY BE AN **ALPHA-LEVEL** MUTANT, **SCOTT**.

OH, YEAH?

HEY!

ALL OF A SUDDEN EVERYBODY BECOMES ABUNDANTLY CONSCIOUS OF **LORNA DANE'S** IMPORTANCE. TO WHOM? THAT IS THE QUESTION.

HANK? HANK?!

IT TAKES ABOUT TWO HOURS FOR THE **BLACKBIRD** JET TO ARRIVE IN **SAN FRANCISCO** FROM **NEW YORK**. THIS IS PRECISELY THE AMOUNT OF TIME IT TAKES FOR **HENRY McCOY** AND **BOBBY DRAKE** TO WAKE BACK UP...

...gone...

SHE'S GONE. YOU DON'T UNDERSTAND.

SHE'S AS STRONG AS **MAGNETO**.

LORNA'S LOCATION BURNS WITH INCANDESCENT CLARITY.

THE **X-MEN** STEALTHILY DISPATCH-ED THE RANK-AND-FILE OF THIS EVIL WORKSHOP...

POLARIS... QUEEN OF THE MUTANTS...

WHAT IS HE DOING TO **LORNA**?

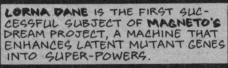

LORNA DANE IS THE FIRST SUC-CESSFUL SUBJECT OF **MAGNETO'S** DREAM PROJECT, A MACHINE THAT ENHANCES LATENT MUTANT GENES INTO SUPER-POWERS.

...DAUGHTER OF **MAGNETO**!

MESMERO'S BEEN ALTERING DANE'S REALITY SINCE **SAN FRANCISCO**.

YOU WILL BE WITH FATHER IN THE **SAVAGE LAND** SOON.

JEAN GREY KNOWS EXACTLY WHAT IS BEING DONE TO THE GIRL.

JEAN MENTALLY PROJECTS A FIGURE FROM HER DREAMS TO DIRECTLY CONVINCE **LORNA** OF THE MANIPULATION TAKING PLACE...

DEEP WITHIN YOUR SOUL YOU KNOW WHAT IS TRUE.

POLARIS?

THE **GAMBIT** DOES ITS JOB.

I DIDN'T KNOW YOU COULD DO THAT, **JEAN**.

LORNA...

NEITHER DID I...

80

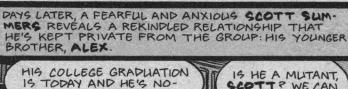
DAYS LATER, A FEARFUL AND ANXIOUS **SCOTT SUMMERS** REVEALS A REKINDLED RELATIONSHIP THAT HE'S KEPT PRIVATE FROM THE GROUP: HIS YOUNGER BROTHER, **ALEX**.

HIS COLLEGE GRADUATION IS TODAY AND HE'S NOWHERE TO BE FOUND.

IS HE A MUTANT, **SCOTT**? WE CAN USE **CEREBRO**!

I... I'M NOT SURE...

THERE'S A 50/50 SHOT GIVEN **SCOTT'S** GENETIC MAKEUP.

ON IT!

KNOWLEDGE OF THE **PHOENIX** IS NOT THE MONOPOLY OF INTERGALACTIC BEINGS. ANCIENT EARTHLY CIVILIZATIONS FORETOLD OF HER IMMENSE POWER.

THE **EGYPTIANS** BELIEVED THAT **PHARAOHS** COULD INFLUENCE THE **PHOENIX FORCE**.

DEEP WITHIN THE **TEMPLE OF HORUS** IN EDFU, EGYPT. THE **LIVING PHARAOH** IS PERFORMING A SACRIFICIAL RITUAL TO SEDUCE THE GREAT **PHOENIX**. BY UNTAPPING THE MUTANT ENERGY OF **ALEX SUMMERS**, THE **PHARAOH** CALLS TO HER.

PROCEDURALLY DURING THE INCANTATION, SOMETHING GOES WRONG.

COMBINING WITH **ALEX SUMMERS'** POWER, THE **LIVING PHARAOH'S** DNA BEGINS TO DANCE THROUGHOUT HIS BODY...

...TRANSFORMING HIM INTO...

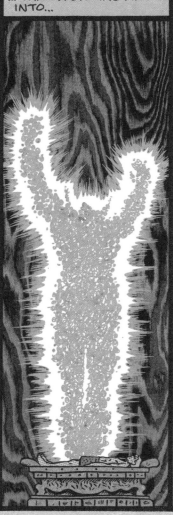

...A **LIVING MONOLITH.**

IT'S HARD TO TELL IF THE **MONOLITH'S** RAPID GROWTH SMASHES A LOAD-BEARING WALL...

...OR IF THE NUCLEAR REACTOR KNOWN AS **ALEX SUMMERS** IS RESPONSIBLE FOR CRUMBLING THE ANCIENT STRUCTURE.

THE OUTBURST ESTABLISHES THE PRIME LOCATION FOR THE **X-MEN** TO BEGIN THEIR INVESTIGATION INTO **SUMMERS'** WHEREABOUTS.

...ALEX...

NOT ONLY DO THE **XAVIER** STUDENTS DEFY **S.H.I.E.L.D.** ORDERS BY CONTINUING THEIR EXISTING WORK TOGETHER, BUT THEY ALSO ADD A NEW STUDENT IN **LORNA DANE.**

SHE'S TOO INEXPERIENCED TO BE ON THE FRONTLINES WITH THE X-MEN IN **EGYPT.** AT FIRST SHE THINKS THIS IS SIMPLY AN ADMINISTERED TEST FROM HER TEACHERS. IT IS NOT.

THE **X-MEN** CALL THE MANSION FROM THE DESERT TO CHECK **CEREBRO'S** LOGS.

LORNA?!

BOBBY, HANK, TAKE THE **BLACK-BIRD** HOME AND REPORT BACK.

I CAN'T LEAVE HERE UNTIL I FIND MY BROTHER.

ALEX SUMMERS IS, IN FACT, QUITE ALIVE.

HE MAY NOT BE FOR LONG, THOUGH.

LARRY TRASK AND HIS AFFILIATES, **THE RIGHT,** HAVE DESIGNS ON USING MUTANT POWER TO SUSTAIN A SMALL ISLAND RESORT OF THEIRS.

ICEMAN WILL KEEP OUR DRINKS COLD ON **GENOSHA ISLAND.**

GOVERNMENT ACTORS WITHIN **THE RIGHT** GENERATE THE NECESSARY PAPERWORK TO DEEM THEIR CAPTIVES AS ENEMIES OF THE STATE.

UP TO THIS POINT, **SENATOR KELLY** HAS HAD A MOSTLY HANDS-OFF APPROACH.

TRASK, THESE JUST LOOK LIKE NORMAL PEOPLE TO ME.

REGARDLESS, 100% OF THE **MACH II SENTINEL** FLEET IS DISPATCHED TO ACQUIRE NEW TARGETS.

THANKS TO THE CONCENTRATION OF ALPHA-LEVEL MUTANTS, **CEREBRO** DISCOVERS THE INSECURE SENTINEL HEADQUARTERS WITH EASE.

THEY'RE **SCUM**!!

JEAN WANTS LARRY TRASK TO KNOW WHAT HIS CAPTIVES HAVE ENDURED AT ONE TIME OR ANOTHER.

I... I'M MUTATING. NO... **NO**!

SHE DIDN'T EXPECT **LARRY'S** REACTION TO HER MINDGAMES TO BE SO IMPULSIVE.

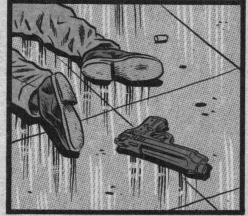

THE FREED **BEAST** AND **CYCLOPS** DISCOVER **MASTER MOLD**, THE MOTHER BRAIN OF THE SENTINEL ROBOTS.

BEAST UPLOADS A SET OF COMMANDS THAT MAKE PERFECT LOGICAL SENSE IN COMPUTER LANGUAGE.

I REROUTED THE ROBOTS TO ATTACK THE VERY CAUSE OF ALL GENETIC MUTATION.

WITH SUDDEN UNIFORMITY, THE ENTIRE CONVOY OF SENTINELS MEET SOMEWHERE IN THE THERMOSPHERE AND BEGIN THEIR COURSE TO THE CENTER OF THE SOLAR SYSTEM.

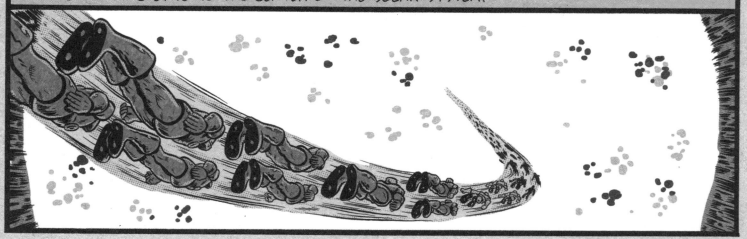

THE **X-MEN** DISCOVER THAT BE-
FORE THWARTING THE SENTINELS,
THE ROBOTS WERE ON THEIR
WAY TO THE **SAVAGE LAND** EN
MASSE AFTER DETECTING A
TITANIC SPIKE IN MUTANT
ACTIVITY.

ANGEL WAS SIMPLY ON A RECONNAISSANCE MISSION BEFORE BEING
INTERCEPTED BY THE HYPNOTIC PTERANO-MAN, **SAURON.**

WARREN'S MISTAKE WAS TO
STARE INTO HIS ADVERSARY'S
EYES FOR TOO LONG.

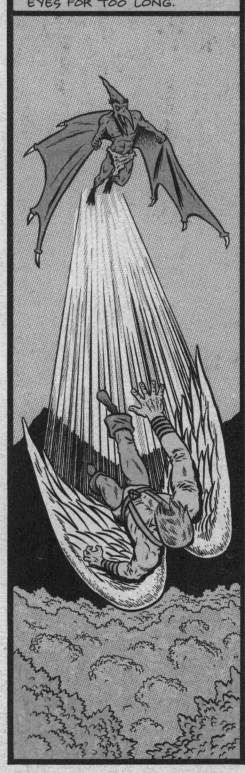

THE FOLIAGE PROVIDED ENOUGH SHOCK-ABSORPTION TO KEEP
WORTHINGTON'S HEART PUMPING, BUT THAT'S ABOUT IT.

ANGELZZZ FROM
THE HEAVENZZZ...

THE **CREATOR**
CAN MAKE HIM ALIVE
HE CAN DO ANYTHING.

ANGEL?!

MY LOVELIES, INVADERS
ARE COMING THIS WAY TO
TRY AND HURT YOUR
DEVOTED **CREATOR!**

I WILL FIGHT THEM
ALONGSIDE YOU EVERY
STEP OF THE WAY.

THE SPACECRAFT **MAGNETO** STOLE FROM **THE STRANGER'S** HOMEWORLD CONTAINED KEY TECHNOLOGY NEEDED TO COMPLETE HIS LONG-SOUGHT-AFTER MUTANT GENE INCUBATOR.

LORELEI IS HIS PRIZED CREATION, AND HER DULCET TONES ARE FAR MORE ENTRANCING THAN WHAT **MASTERMIND** OR **MESMERO** COULD EVER HOPE TO CONJUR UP.

HUH?

GUYS?

MARVEL GIRL HAS HER OWN WAY OF HOLDING SWAY OVER HER COMRADES-IN-ARMS.

AFTER THE MAELSTROM, **JEAN** ISN'T QUITE SURE IF THE CITADEL WAS BROUGHT DOWN ON TOP OF **MAGNETO'S** HEAD OR NOT.

THE FACT REMAINS, WHENEVER OUTWORLDERS ENTER THE **SAVAGE LAND**, DEATH AND DESTRUCTION FOLLOW.

LEAVE.

86

THE **X-MEN** KNOW TO EXPECT VERY LITTLE DOWN-TIME IN BETWEEN MISSIONS.

I'M BACK, MY STUDENTS, AND IT'S TIME WE ADDRESS A VAST ENEMY.

"**MUTANT MASTER'S** ARMADA SHOWS NO EVIDENCE OF BACKING DOWN. IN FACT, THEY'RE NOW CLOSE ENOUGH TO **EARTH** THAT WE CAN DO SOMETHING ABOUT IT."

PROFESSOR X DEDICATED MANY MONTHS TO A PLAN. **FORGE** FABRICATED A SUIT FOR **ALEX SUMMERS** TO HARNESS ALL HIS ENERGY SO IT CAN BE USED TO SUPERCHARGE HIS BROTHER **CYCLOPS'** OPTIC BLAST. **ICEMAN** HELPS REGULATE **SCOTT SUMMERS'** BLISTERING BODY TEMPERATURE.

XAVIER CRISSCROSSED THE GLOBE BUILDING A PSYCHIC NETWORK WITH THE STRONGEST BEINGS ON THE PLANET. **JEAN GREY** HELPS BOOST MENTAL CONTACT TO DIRECT THEIR COLLECTIVE CONSCIOUSNESS TO THE LASER-LIKE FOCAL POINT **CYCLOPS** IS BEAMING TOWARD THE COSMOS.

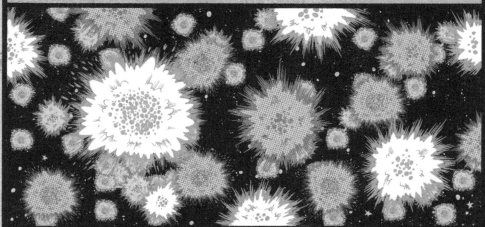

THE ALIEN FLEET DOESN'T STAND A CHANCE AGAINST THE TYPHOON OF THOUGHT-POWER CONCENTRATED DIRECTLY FROM EARTH.

THE STRAIN ZAPS ALL OF THE PROFESSOR'S ENERGY, LEAVING HIM SICK, ANEMIC AND COMATOSE.

PROFESSOR?

ON THE UNCONSCIOUS PLANE, **XAVIER'S** MIND FILLS WITH INDECIPHERABLE VISIONS.

JEAN TAKES A BIG RISK TO GET HER MENTOR OUT OF HIS SLEEP. IT WORKS.

Krakoa...

KRAKOA...

PROFESSOR.

YOU HAD US WORRIED.

KRAKOA?

PULSE IS NORMAL.

REST EASY, PROFESSOR.

BIG ...

...TROUBLE...

WE'VE BEEN KEEPING UP WITH OUR **DANGER ROOM** REGIMEN, SIR.

OH, **SCOTT.**

AND SO THEY FOUGHT HAPPILY EVER AFTER, **WATCHER?**

PLEASE, **RECORDER**. OF COURSE I HAVE **MANY** MORE OBSERVATIONS THAT REQUIRE TRANSCRIPTION.

UNTIL THE UNIVERSE BLINKS OUT, THERE IS ALWAYS MORE TO THE STORY...

NEVER THE END...

DREAM PROJECT!!

LEFT: **ED PISKOR** (GREEN SHIRT), AGE 7, AND COUSIN FRUSTRATED WHILE PLAYING THE **X-MEN** GAME FOR THE **NINTENDO ENTERTAINMENT SYSTEM.**

ABOVE: THE BATTERED REMNANTS OF **ED'S** TOY COLLECTION EXCAVATED FROM HIS FOLKS' HOUSE.

PISKOR'S PLAN WAS ALWAYS TO GROW UP AND MAKE COMIC BOOKS. HIS MOTHER, AN ARTIST IN HER OWN RIGHT, RECOGNIZED **ED'S** INTEREST IN DRAWING AND DID WHAT SHE COULD TO SHOW HIM THE ROPES. EARLY ON, HIS FAVORITE PAST TIME WAS COPYING DRAWINGS FROM **X-MEN** COMICS WITH HER.

STEVEN BUTLER COVER DETAIL. THE OFFICIAL MARVEL INDEX TO THE X-MEN, VOL. 2, NO. 1, 1994

MOMMA PISKOR'S TAKE ON THE BLOB.

LITTLE **EDDIE PISKOR'S** INTERPRETATION.

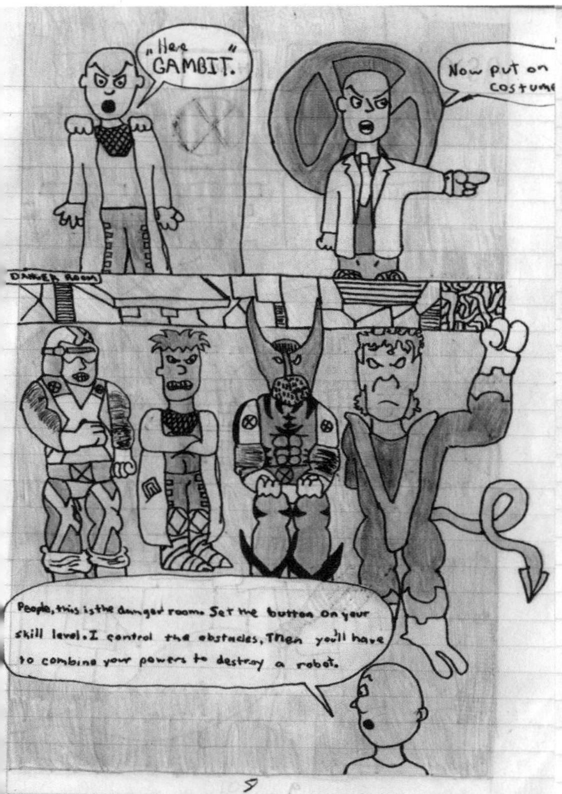
"Here GAMBIT."
Now put on costume
DANGER ROOM
People, this is the danger room. Set the button on your skill level. I control the obstacles, Then you'll have to combine your powers to destroy a robot.

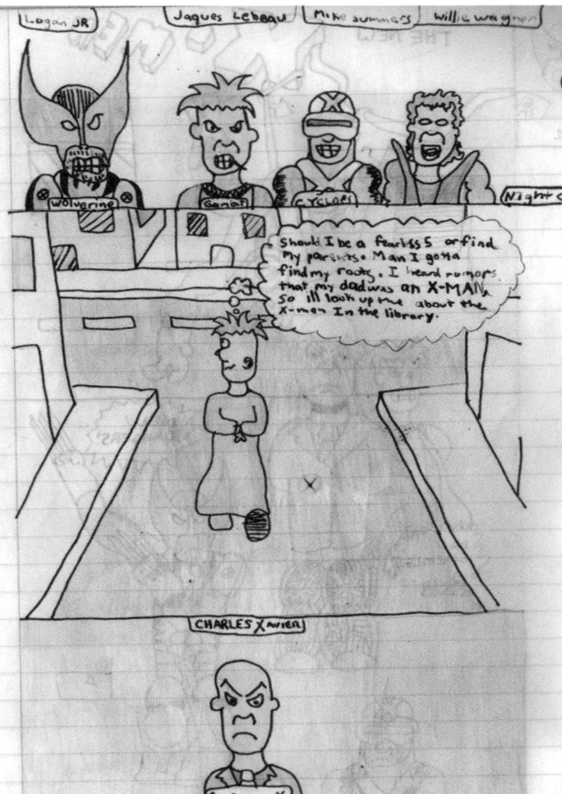
Logan JR
Jaques Lebeau
Mike summers
willie wagner
wolverine
Gambit
Cyclops
Night c
Should I be a fearless 5 or find my parents. Man I gotta find my roots. I heard rumors that my dad was an X-MAN, so ill look up the about the X-men In the library.
CHARLES XAVIER

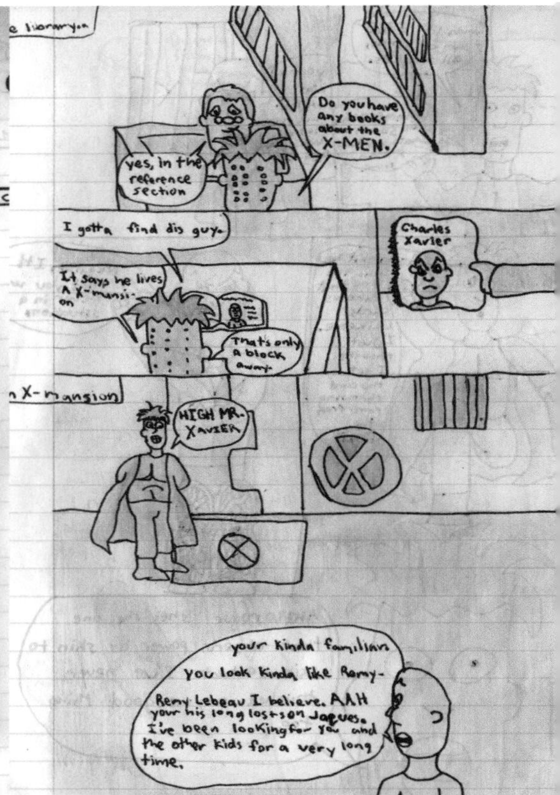
e library..
Do you have any books about the X-MEN.
yes, in the reference section
I gotta find dis guy.
It says he lives A X-mansion
Charles Xavier
That's only a block away.
n X-mansion
HIGH MR. XAVIER
your kinda familiar. You look kinda like Remy- Remy Lebeau I believe. AAH your his long lost son Jaques. I've been looking for you and the other kids for a very long time.

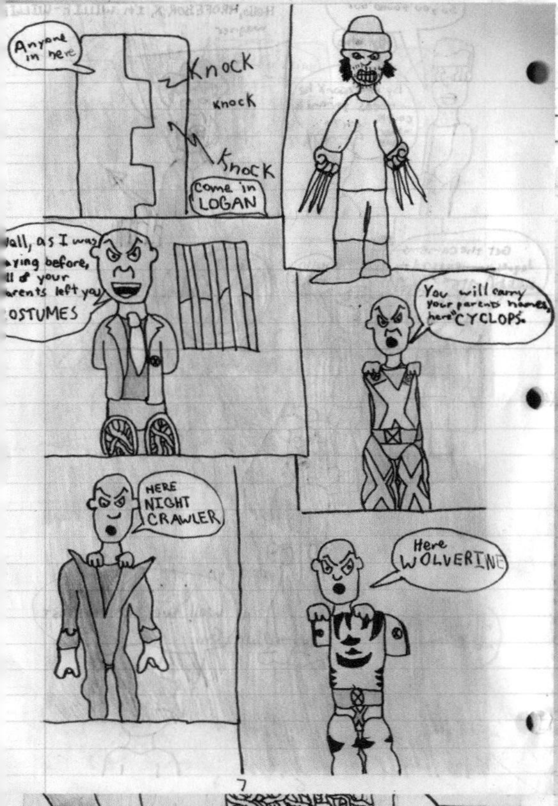
Anyone in here
Knock
knock
knock
Come in LOGAN
Well, as I was saying before, all of your parents left you COSTUMES
You will carry your parents names, here" CYCLOPS.
HERE NIGHT CRAWLER
Here WOLVERINE

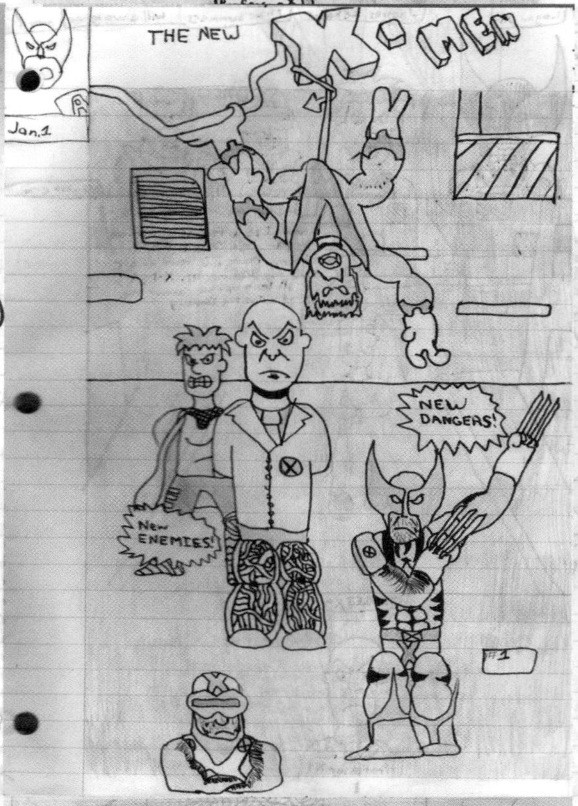
THE NEW X-MEN
Jan.1
NEW DANGERS!
New ENEMIES!
#1

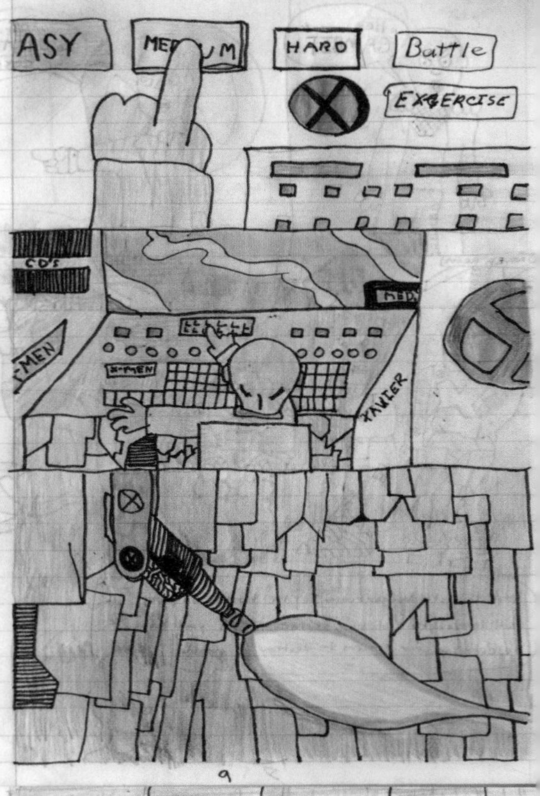
ASY
MEDIUM
HARD
Battle
EXERCISE
CD's
X-MEN
XAVIER

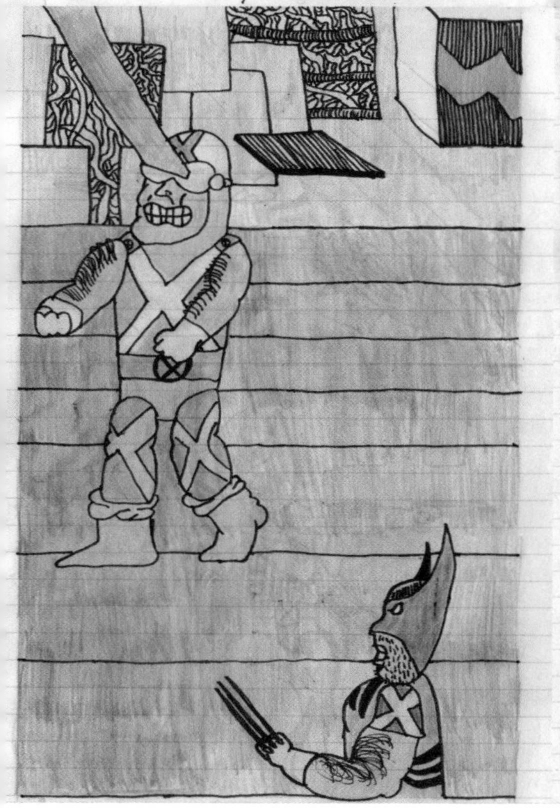

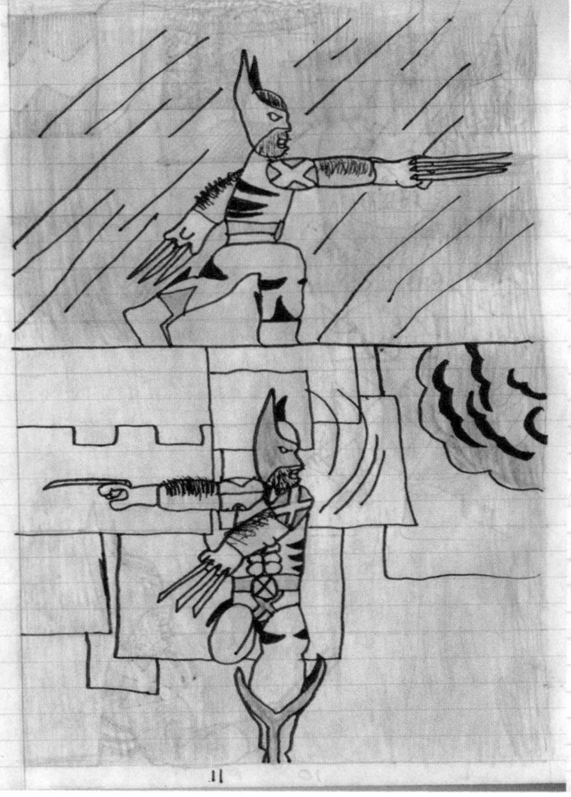

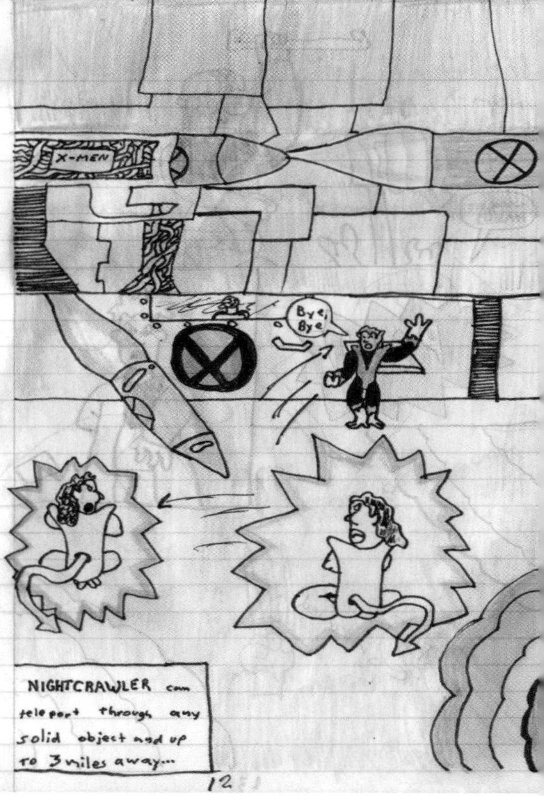
X-MEN
Bye, Bye
NIGHTCRAWLER can teleport through any solid object and up to 3 miles away...

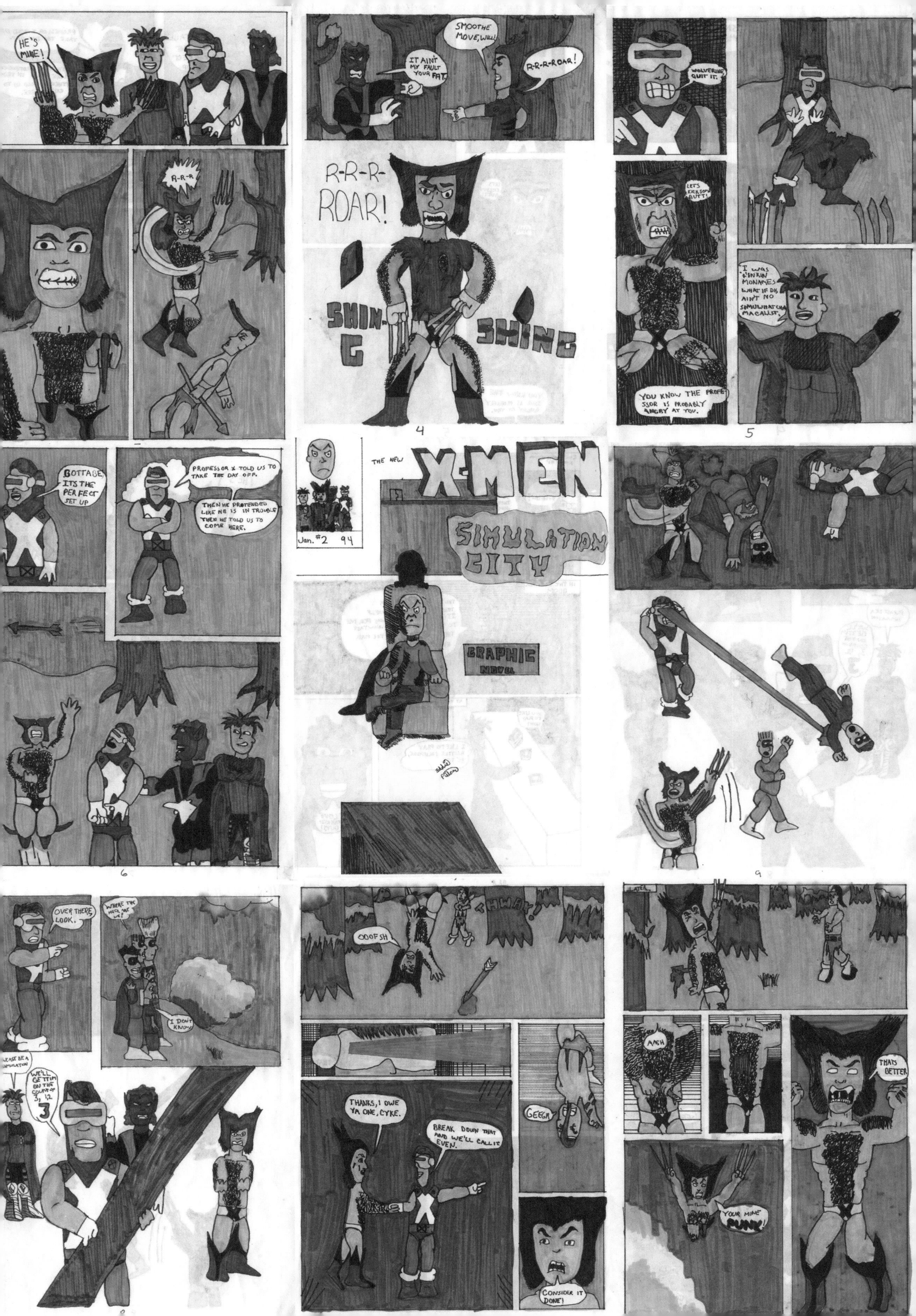
HE'S MINE!
R-R-R
SMOOTHE MOVE, WILL!
IT AIN'T MY FAULT YOUR FAT.
R-R-R-ROAR!
R-R-R-ROAR!
SHIN-G
SHING
4
WOLVERINE QUIT IT.
LET'S KICKSOME BUTT!
YOU KNOW THE PROFESSOR IS PROBABLY ANGRY AT YOU.
I WAS THINKIN MONAMES WHAT IF DIS AIN'T NO SIMULWHATCHA MACALLIT.
5
GOTTA BE, ITS THE PERFECT SET UP
PROFESSOR X TOLD US TO TAKE THE DAY OFF.
THEN HE PROTENDED LIKE HE IS IN TROUBLE THEN HE TOLD US TO COME HERE.
6
Jan. #2 94
THE NEW
X-MEN
SIMULATION CITY
GRAPHIC NOVEL
9
OVER THERE LOOK.
WHERE THE HECK ARE WE?
I DON'T KNOW
PLEASE BE A SIMULATION
WE'LL GET HIM ON THE COUNT OF 3, 1, 2 3
THWAK!
OOOFSH
GEEGH
THANKS, I OWE YA ONE, CYKE.
BREAK DOWN THAT AND WE'LL CALL IT EVEN.
CONSIDER IT DONE!
LATER...
AAGH
THATS BETTER
YOUR MINE PUNK!

PREVIOUS TWO PAGES: **PISKOR** DREW OVER 1,000 PAGES OF COMICS AS A LAD, MANY OF THEM WERE **X-MEN** COMICS.

RIGHT AND BELOW: SADLY, ONLY THE COVERS TO THESE ISSUES STILL EXIST.

BOTTOM: WHAT PASSED FOR A DYNAMIC TEAM SHOT CONTAINING ALL OF **ED'S** FAVORITE CHARACTERS FROM THAT TIME.

PISKOR IS AN O.G. **DEADPOOL** FAN FROM WAY BACK.

TEENAGE EDDIE P. WAS HEAVY-HANDED AND RARELY FINISHED THINGS.

BELOW: AN ASSIGNMENT FROM **ED'S** ONE YEAR AT THE **KUBERT SCHOOL**.

BELOW: A PIECE OF FAN ART THAT LED TO THIS BOOK'S CREATION.

XAVIER'S SCHOOL
FOR GIFTED YOUNGSTERS

 SUMMA CUM LAUDE
For their service in shaping the
first 30 years of X-MEN history
to make this book possible.

ART ADAMS
NEAL ADAMS
DAN ADKINS
DIANA ALBERS
KARL ALTSTAETTER
BILL ANDERSON
BRENT ANDERSON
ROSS ANDRU
TERRY AUSTIN
DICK AYERS
MICHAEL BAIR
HILARY BARTA
BRET BLEVINS
PAT BLEVINS
JOHN BOLTON
BRETT BREEDING
JUNE BRIDGMAN
SOL BRODSKY
PAT BROSSEAU
BOB BROWN
ELIOT R. BROWN
RICH BUCKLER
BOB BUDIANSKY
LOIS BUHALIS
JOHN BUSCEMA
SAL BUSCEMA
JOHN BYRNE
JANINE CASEY
JANICE CHIANG
FRANK CHIARAMONTE
CHRIS CLAREMONT
DAVE COCKRUM
JANICE COHEN
VINCE COLLETTA
MIKE COLLINS
HERB COOPER
JOHN COSTANZA
P. CRAIG RUSSELL
DAN CRESPI
KEVIN CUNNINGHAM
ALAN DAVIS
SAM De La ROSA
TONY DeZUNIGA
ARNOLD DRAKE
KIERON DWYER
DARYL EDELMAN
CHRIS ELIOPOULOS
MIKE ESPOSITO
JERRY FELDMANN
DANNY FINGEROTH
GARY FRIEDRICH
SUZANNE GAFFNEY
KERRY GAMMILL
FRANK GIACOIA
PETRA GOLDBERG
STAN GOLDBERG
MICHAEL GOLDEN

ARCHIE GOODWIN
AL GORDON
SAM GRAINGER
DAN GREEN
JACKSON GUICE
BOB HARRAS
DON HECK
MICHAEL HEISLER
PETER IRO
BILL JAASKA
KLAUS JANSON
GIL KANE
TERRY KAVANAGH
ANNETTE KAWECKI
JACK KIRBY
ANDY KUBERT
MORRIE KURAMOTO
BOB LAYTON
JIM LEE
STAN LEE
STEVE LEIALOHA
RICK LEONARDI
ROB LIEFELD
KEN LOPEZ
TOM MANDRAKE
KAREN MANTLO
BOB McLEOD
MIKE MIGNOLA
AL MILGROM
FRANK MILLER
FRANCOISE MOULY
PAUL NEARY
FABIAN NICIEZA
ANN NOCENTI
JIM NOVAK
KEVIN NOWLAN
GLYNIS OLIVER (WEIN)
TOM ORZECHOWSKI
TOM PALMER
RICK PARKER
BRUCE PATTERSON
GEORGE PEREZ
WHILCE PORTACIO
SUZANNE R. A. MILLER
PHIL RACHELSON
TOM RANEY
PAUL REINMAN
CLEM ROBBINS
TRINA ROBBINS
MIKE ROCKWITZ
JOHN ROMITA JR
JOHN ROMITA
JOE ROSAS
JOE ROSEN
SAM ROSEN
WERNER ROTH
GEORGE ROUSSOS

JOSEF RUBINSTEIN
TOMOKO SAITO
GASPAR SALADINO
JIM SALICRUP
PETER SANDERSON
CHRISTIE SCHEELE
PETRA SCOTESE
MARIE SEVERIN
BOB SHAREN
JIM SHERMAN
JIM SHOOTER
BILL SIENKIEWICZ
MARC SILVESTRI
ART SIMEK
JEAN SIMEK
LOUISE SIMONSON (JONES)
WALT SIMONSON
JOE SINNOTT
PAUL SMITH
JIM STERANKO
ROGER STERN
CHIC STONE
LARRY STROMAN
TOM SUTTON
JOHN TARTAGLIONE
ART THIBERT
ROY THOMAS
MARY TITUS
ALEX TOTH
HERB TRIMPE
GEORGE TUSKA
BRAD VANCATA
JOHN VERPOORTEN
RICARDO VILLAMONTE
TOM VINCENT
MIKE VOSBERG
DON WARFIELD
IRVING WATANABE
LEN WEIN
BOB WIACEK
BONNIE WILFORD
KENT WILLIAMS
SCOTT WILLIAMS
AL WILLIAMSON
BARRY WINDSOR-SMITH
DENISE WOHL
MARV WOLFMAN
MICHELLE WOLFMAN
WALLACE WOOD
BILL WRAY
GREG WRIGHT
ANDY YANCHUS
RON ZALME

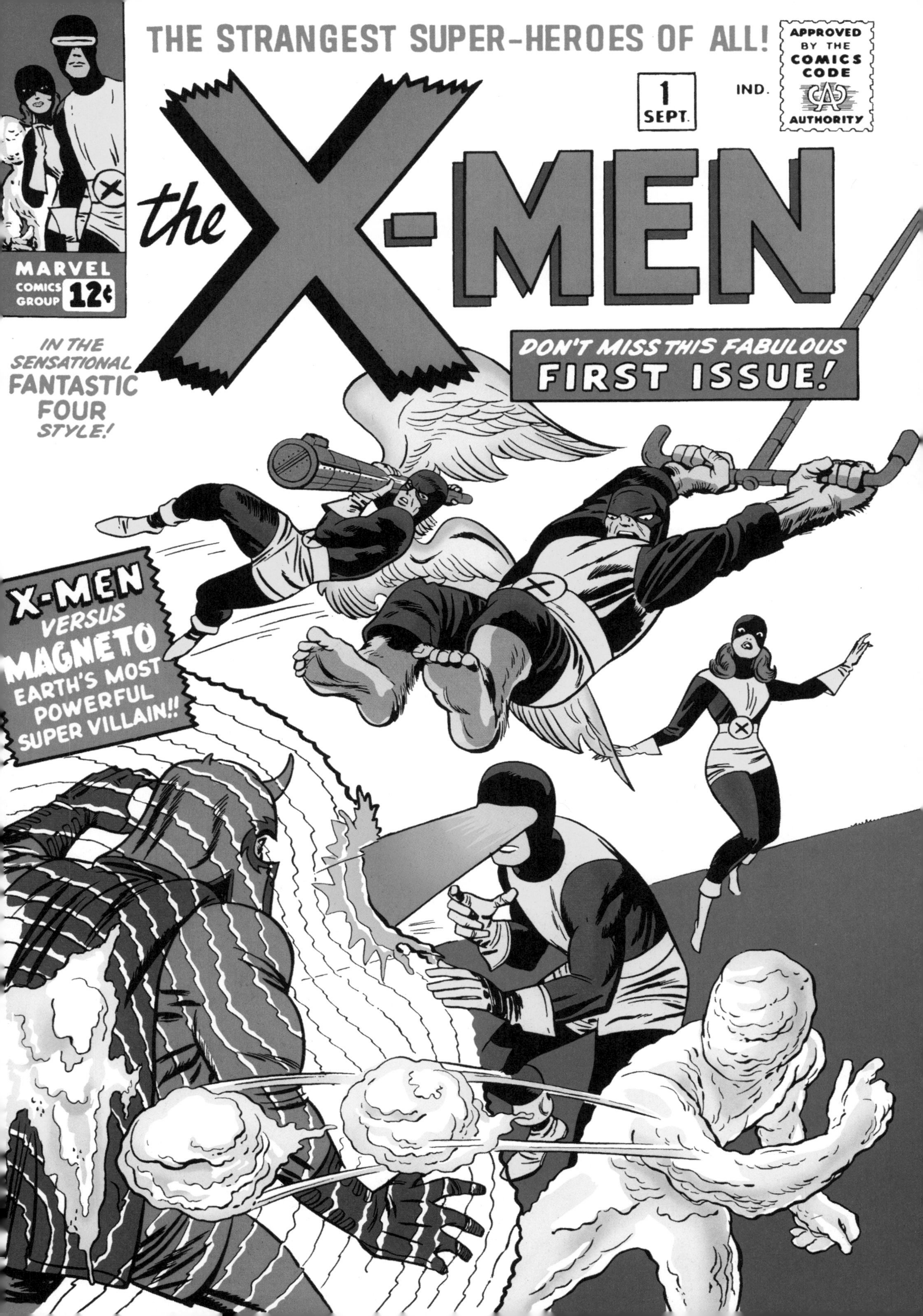
THE STRANGEST SUPER-HEROES OF ALL!
APPROVED BY THE COMICS CODE AUTHORITY
1 SEPT.
IND.
MARVEL COMICS GROUP 12¢
the X-MEN
DON'T MISS THIS FABULOUS FIRST ISSUE!
IN THE SENSATIONAL FANTASTIC FOUR STYLE!
X-MEN VERSUS MAGNETO EARTH'S MOST POWERFUL SUPER VILLAIN!!

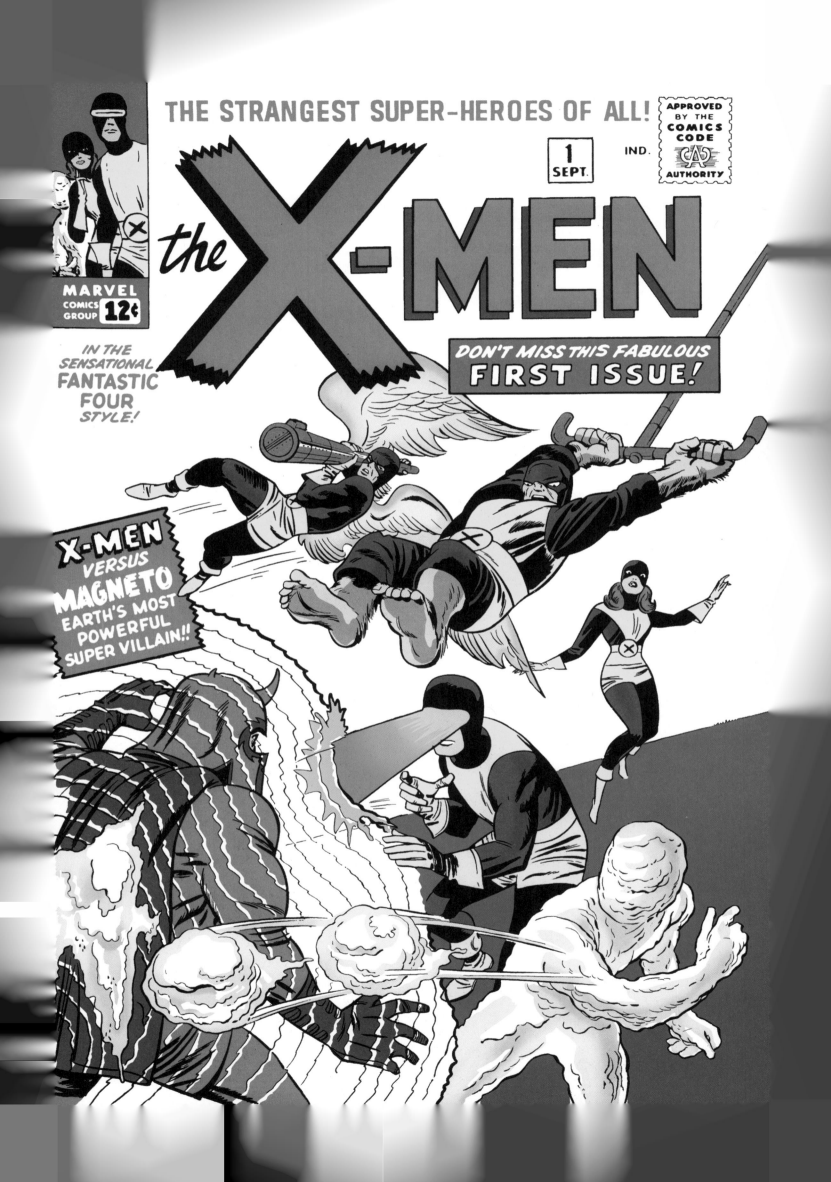

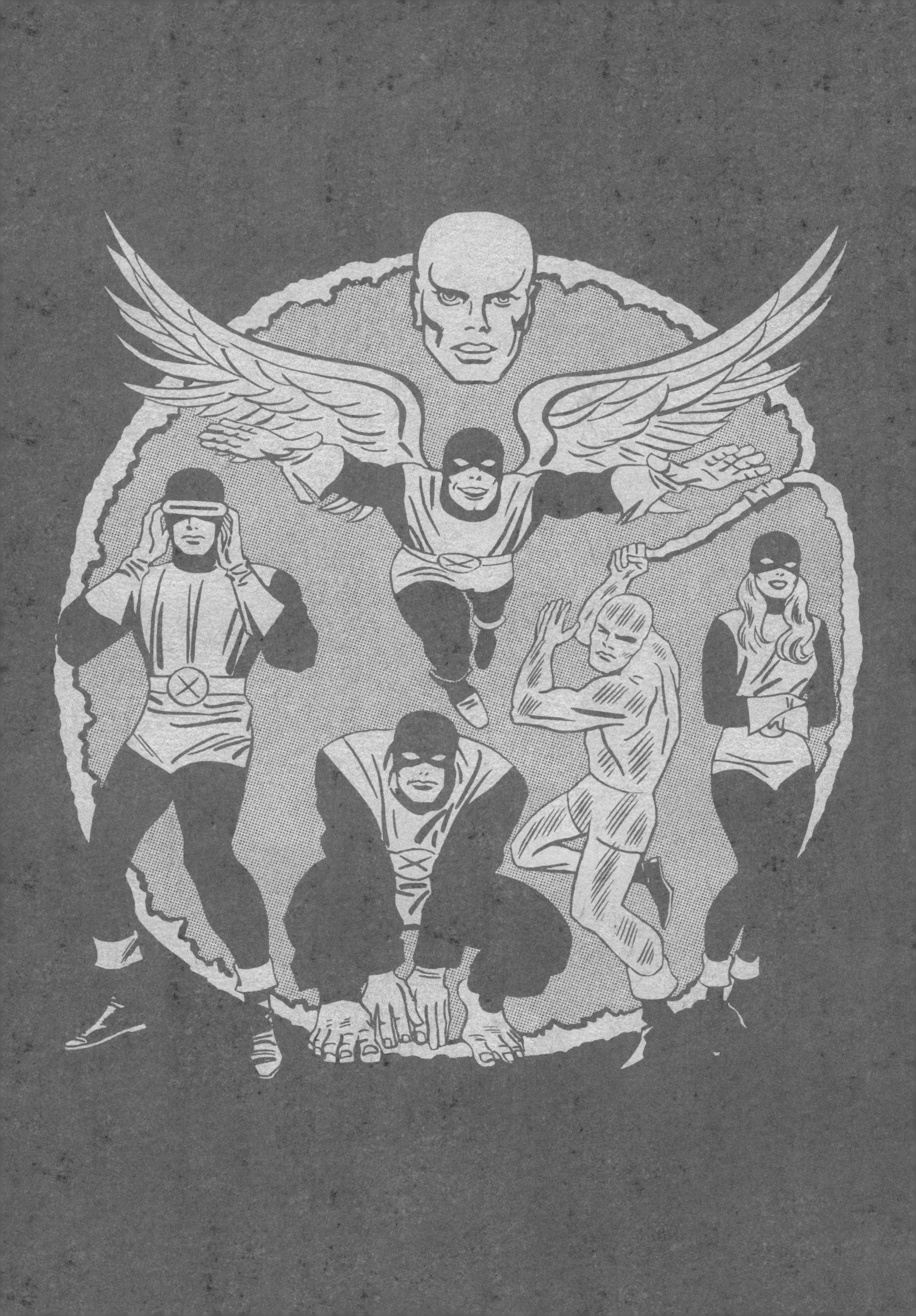

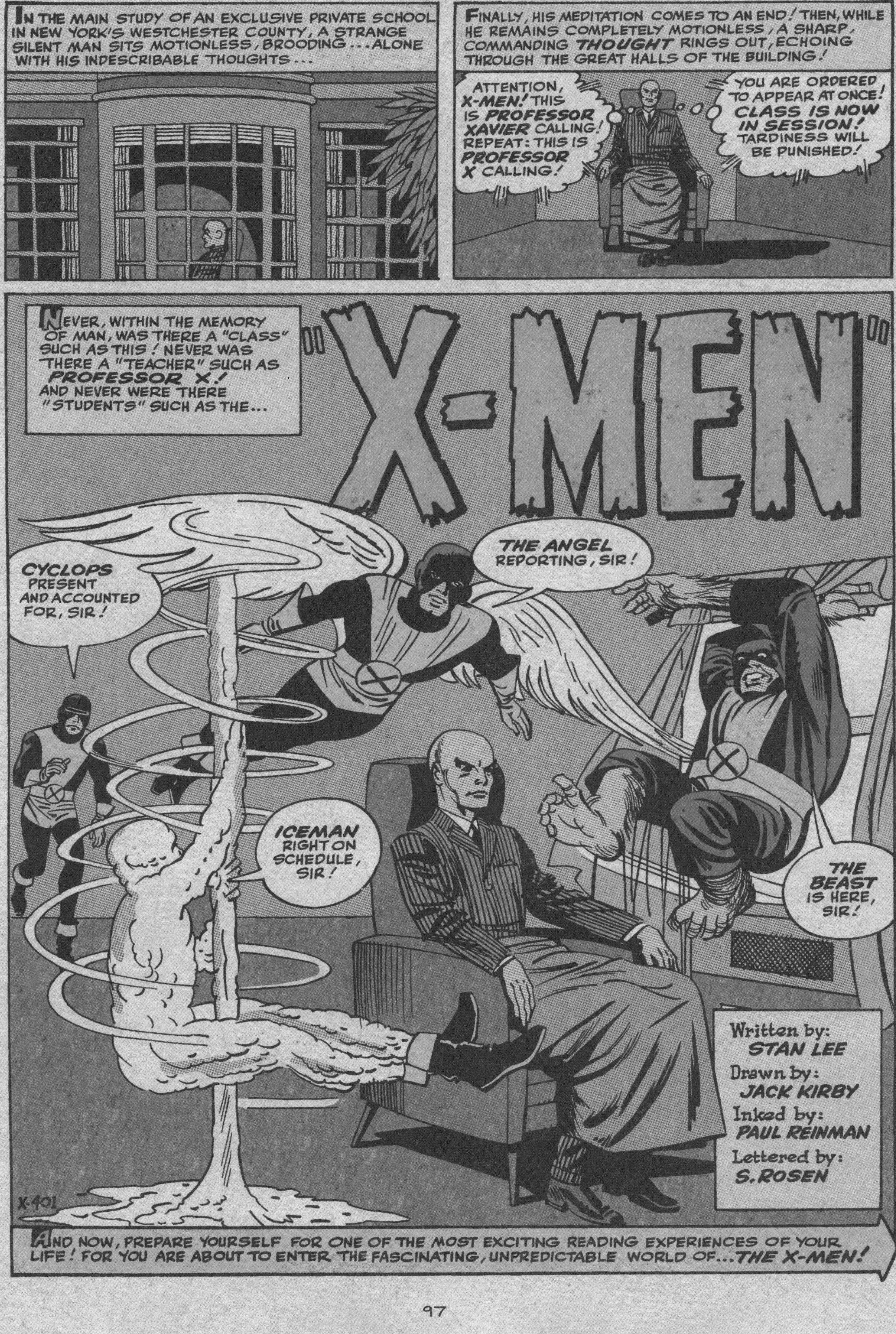
IN THE MAIN STUDY OF AN EXCLUSIVE PRIVATE SCHOOL IN NEW YORK'S WESTCHESTER COUNTY, A STRANGE SILENT MAN SITS MOTIONLESS, BROODING... ALONE WITH HIS INDESCRIBABLE THOUGHTS...
FINALLY, HIS MEDITATION COMES TO AN END! THEN, WHILE HE REMAINS COMPLETELY MOTIONLESS, A SHARP, COMMANDING THOUGHT RINGS OUT, ECHOING THROUGH THE GREAT HALLS OF THE BUILDING!
ATTENTION, X-MEN! THIS IS PROFESSOR XAVIER CALLING! REPEAT: THIS IS PROFESSOR X CALLING!
YOU ARE ORDERED TO APPEAR AT ONCE! CLASS IS NOW IN SESSION! TARDINESS WILL BE PUNISHED!
NEVER, WITHIN THE MEMORY OF MAN, WAS THERE A "CLASS" SUCH AS THIS! NEVER WAS THERE A "TEACHER" SUCH AS PROFESSOR X! AND NEVER WERE THERE "STUDENTS" SUCH AS THE...
"X-MEN"
CYCLOPS PRESENT AND ACCOUNTED FOR, SIR!
THE ANGEL REPORTING, SIR!
ICEMAN RIGHT ON SCHEDULE, SIR!
THE BEAST IS HERE, SIR!
Written by: STAN LEE
Drawn by: JACK KIRBY
Inked by: PAUL REINMAN
Lettered by: S. ROSEN
X-401
AND NOW, PREPARE YOURSELF FOR ONE OF THE MOST EXCITING READING EXPERIENCES OF YOUR LIFE! FOR YOU ARE ABOUT TO ENTER THE FASCINATING, UNPREDICTABLE WORLD OF... THE X-MEN!

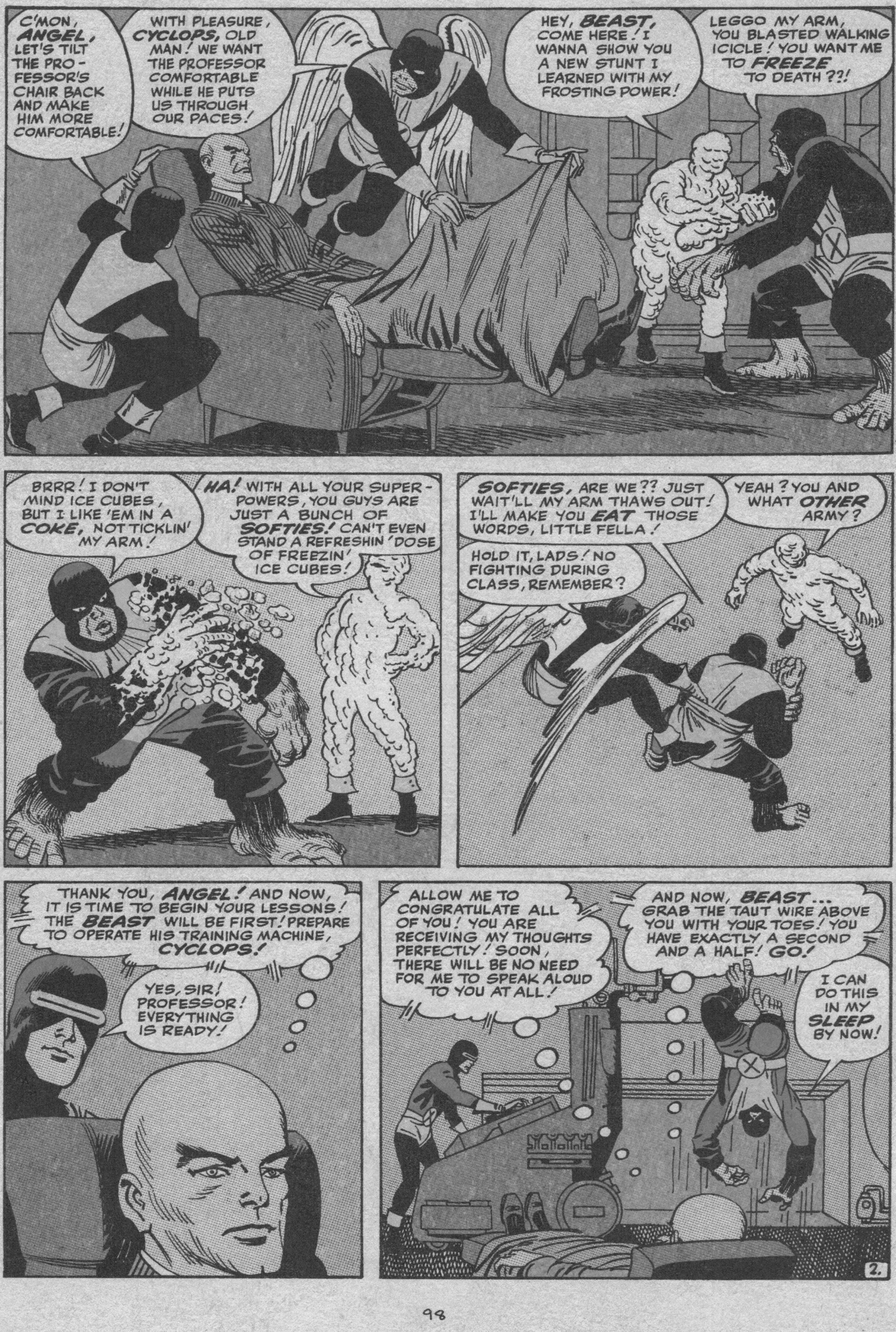
C'MON, ANGEL, LET'S TILT THE PRO-FESSOR'S CHAIR BACK AND MAKE HIM MORE COMFORTABLE!
WITH PLEASURE, CYCLOPS, OLD MAN! WE WANT THE PROFESSOR COMFORTABLE WHILE HE PUTS US THROUGH OUR PACES!
HEY, BEAST, COME HERE! I WANNA SHOW YOU A NEW STUNT I LEARNED WITH MY FROSTING POWER!
LEGGO MY ARM, YOU BLASTED WALKING ICICLE! YOU WANT ME TO FREEZE TO DEATH??!
BRRR! I DON'T MIND ICE CUBES, BUT I LIKE 'EM IN A COKE, NOT TICKLIN' MY ARM!
HA! WITH ALL YOUR SUPER-POWERS, YOU GUYS ARE JUST A BUNCH OF SOFTIES! CAN'T EVEN STAND A REFRESHIN' DOSE OF FREEZIN' ICE CUBES!
SOFTIES, ARE WE?? JUST WAIT'LL MY ARM THAWS OUT! I'LL MAKE YOU EAT THOSE WORDS, LITTLE FELLA!
YEAH? YOU AND WHAT OTHER ARMY?
HOLD IT, LADS! NO FIGHTING DURING CLASS, REMEMBER?
THANK YOU, ANGEL! AND NOW, IT IS TIME TO BEGIN YOUR LESSONS! THE BEAST WILL BE FIRST! PREPARE TO OPERATE HIS TRAINING MACHINE, CYCLOPS!
YES, SIR! PROFESSOR! EVERYTHING IS READY!
ALLOW ME TO CONGRATULATE ALL OF YOU! YOU ARE RECEIVING MY THOUGHTS PERFECTLY! SOON, THERE WILL BE NO NEED FOR ME TO SPEAK ALOUD TO YOU AT ALL!
AND NOW, BEAST... GRAB THE TAUT WIRE ABOVE YOU WITH YOUR TOES! YOU HAVE EXACTLY A SECOND AND A HALF! GO!
I CAN DO THIS IN MY SLEEP BY NOW!
2.

EXCELLENT! NOW SPIN AROUND! FASTER! FASTER! PRETEND AN ENEMY IS SHOOTING AT YOU! YOU MUST MAKE YOURSELF AN IMPOSSIBLE TARGET!

AND NOW, AT MY COMMAND, RELEASE YOURSELF FROM THE TAUT WIRE AND EXECUTE MANEUVER "G"! YOU HAVE EXACTLY THREE SECONDS!

GO!

THREE SECONDS EXACTLY! WELL DONE, BEAST!

NOW FOR YOUR BALANCE DRILL! STEADY... STEADY! SLACKEN THE TENSION, CYCLOPS!

GOOD.!! NOW, AS THE ROD BEGINS TO SAG, MAINTAIN YOUR BALANCE... ON ONE FINGER! HOLD IT! HOLD IT!

TOO FAST! YOU'RE SWAYING TOO MUCH! RECOVER... QUICKLY! NOW LAND ON YOUR FEET BEFORE THE ROD SNAPS BACK! CAREFUL... CAREFUL...

WHEW... HOW'D I DO, SIR?

YOU'LL RECEIVE YOUR GRADE TOMORROW! ALL RIGHT, ANGEL... IT'S YOUR TURN!

ARE YOU RECEIVING MY THOUGHT CLEARLY? GOOD! NOW, BE SHARP... TODAY WE TEST YOUR WING REFLEX! YOU DARE NOT MAKE A MISTAKE!

MISTAKES ARE FOR HOMO SAPIENS, SIR... NOT THE ANGEL!

3.

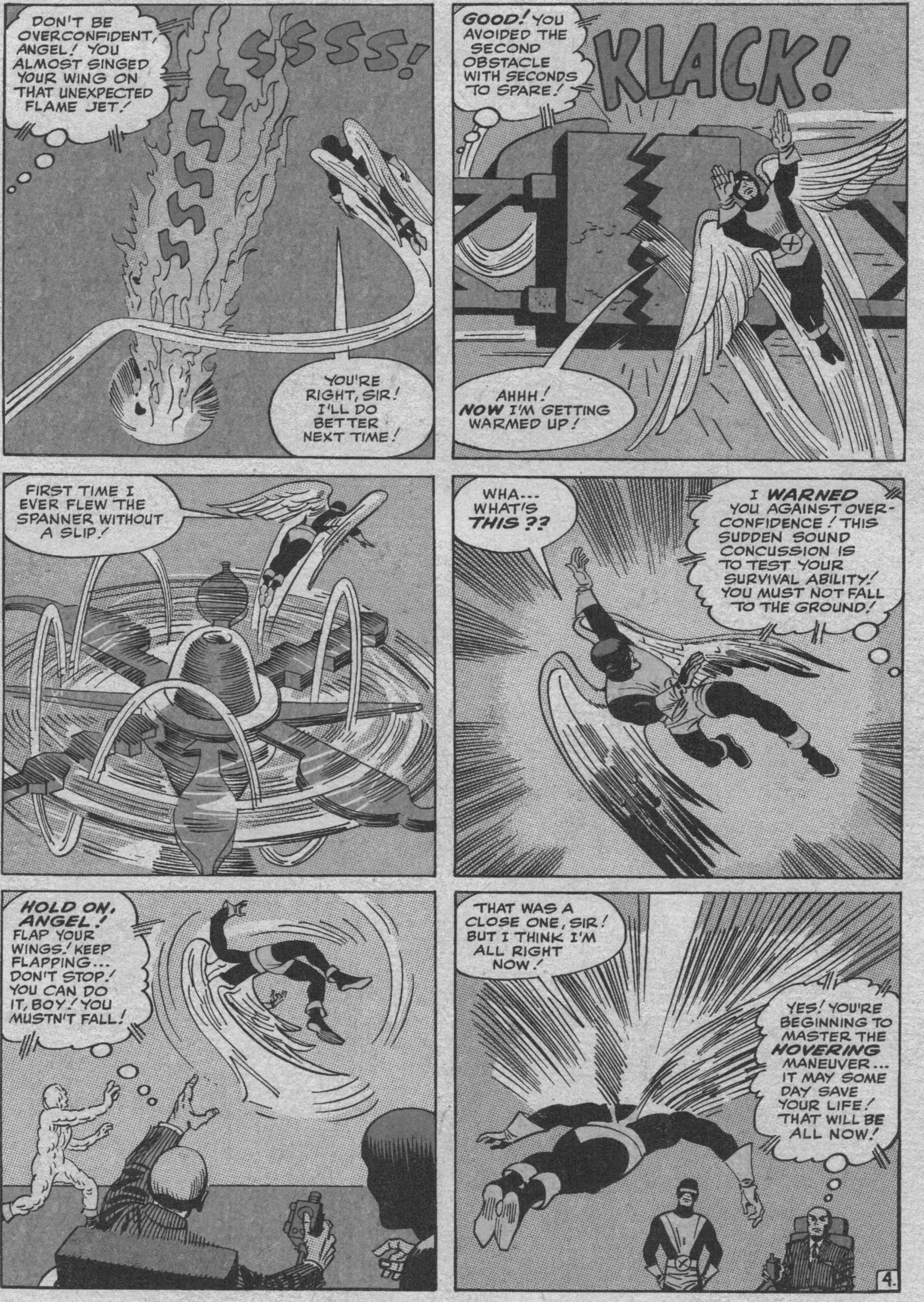
DON'T BE OVERCONFIDENT, ANGEL! YOU ALMOST SINGED YOUR WING ON THAT UNEXPECTED FLAME JET!
SSSSS!
YOU'RE RIGHT, SIR! I'LL DO BETTER NEXT TIME!
GOOD! YOU AVOIDED THE SECOND OBSTACLE WITH SECONDS TO SPARE!
KLACK!
AHHH! NOW I'M GETTING WARMED UP!
FIRST TIME I EVER FLEW THE SPANNER WITHOUT A SLIP!
WHA... WHAT'S THIS??
I WARNED YOU AGAINST OVER-CONFIDENCE! THIS SUDDEN SOUND CONCUSSION IS TO TEST YOUR SURVIVAL ABILITY! YOU MUST NOT FALL TO THE GROUND!
HOLD ON, ANGEL! FLAP YOUR WINGS! KEEP FLAPPING... DON'T STOP! YOU CAN DO IT, BOY! YOU MUSTN'T FALL!
THAT WAS A CLOSE ONE, SIR! BUT I THINK I'M ALL RIGHT NOW!
YES! YOU'RE BEGINNING TO MASTER THE HOVERING MANEUVER... IT MAY SOME DAY SAVE YOUR LIFE! THAT WILL BE ALL NOW!
4.

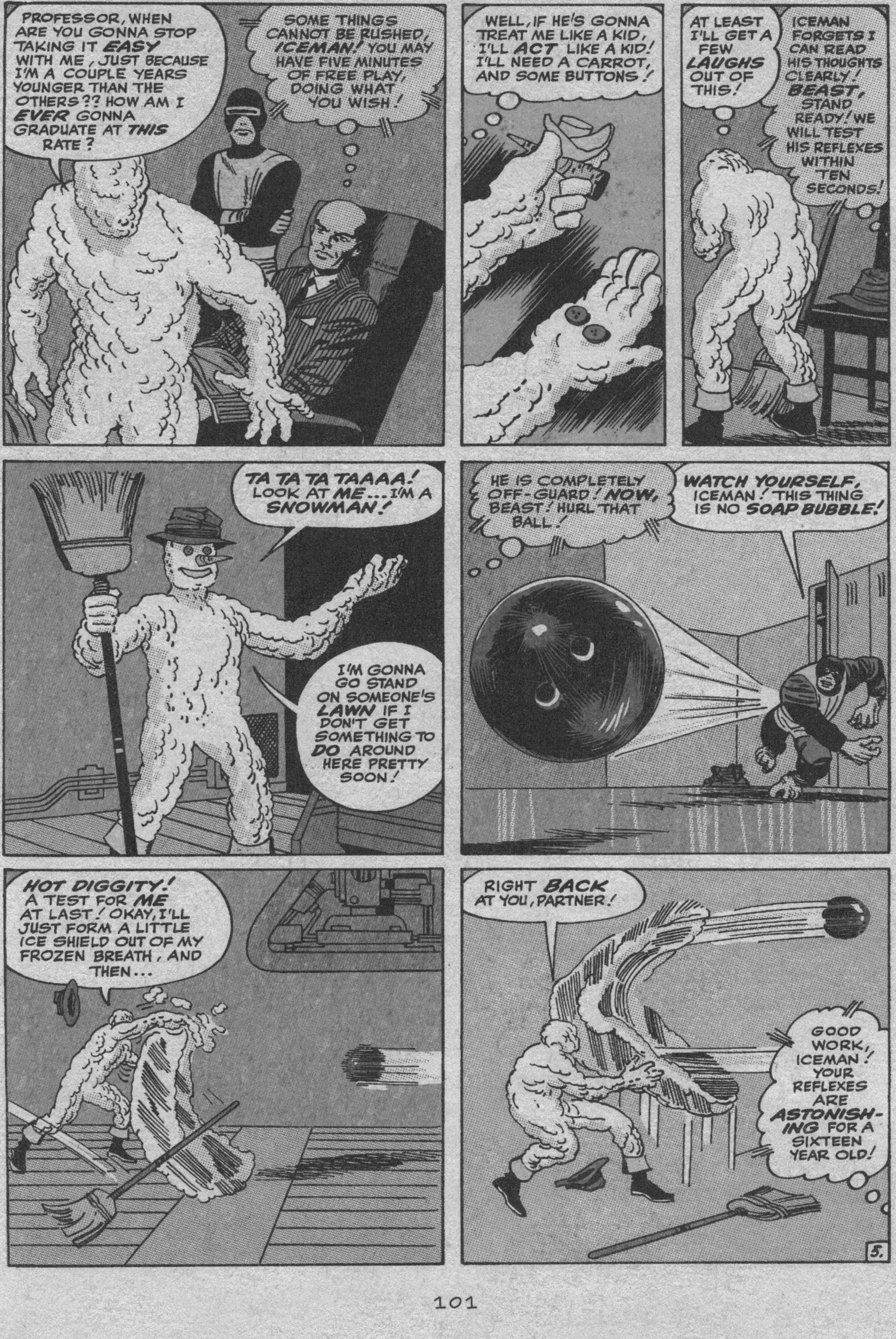
PROFESSOR, WHEN ARE YOU GONNA STOP TAKING IT EASY WITH ME, JUST BECAUSE I'M A COUPLE YEARS YOUNGER THAN THE OTHERS?? HOW AM I EVER GONNA GRADUATE AT THIS RATE?
SOME THINGS CANNOT BE RUSHED, ICEMAN! YOU MAY HAVE FIVE MINUTES OF FREE PLAY, DOING WHAT YOU WISH!
WELL, IF HE'S GONNA TREAT ME LIKE A KID, I'LL ACT LIKE A KID! I'LL NEED A CARROT, AND SOME BUTTONS!
AT LEAST I'LL GET A FEW LAUGHS OUT OF THIS!
ICEMAN FORGETS I CAN READ HIS THOUGHTS CLEARLY! BEAST, STAND READY! WE WILL TEST HIS REFLEXES WITHIN TEN SECONDS!
TA TA TA TAAAA! LOOK AT ME... I'M A SNOWMAN!
I'M GONNA GO STAND ON SOMEONE'S LAWN IF I DON'T GET SOMETHING TO DO AROUND HERE PRETTY SOON!
HE IS COMPLETELY OFF-GUARD! NOW, BEAST! HURL THAT BALL!
WATCH YOURSELF, ICEMAN! THIS THING IS NO SOAP BUBBLE!
HOT DIGGITY! A TEST FOR ME AT LAST! OKAY, I'LL JUST FORM A LITTLE ICE SHIELD OUT OF MY FROZEN BREATH, AND THEN...
RIGHT BACK AT YOU, PARTNER!
GOOD WORK, ICEMAN! YOUR REFLEXES ARE ASTONISHING FOR A SIXTEEN YEAR OLD!
5.

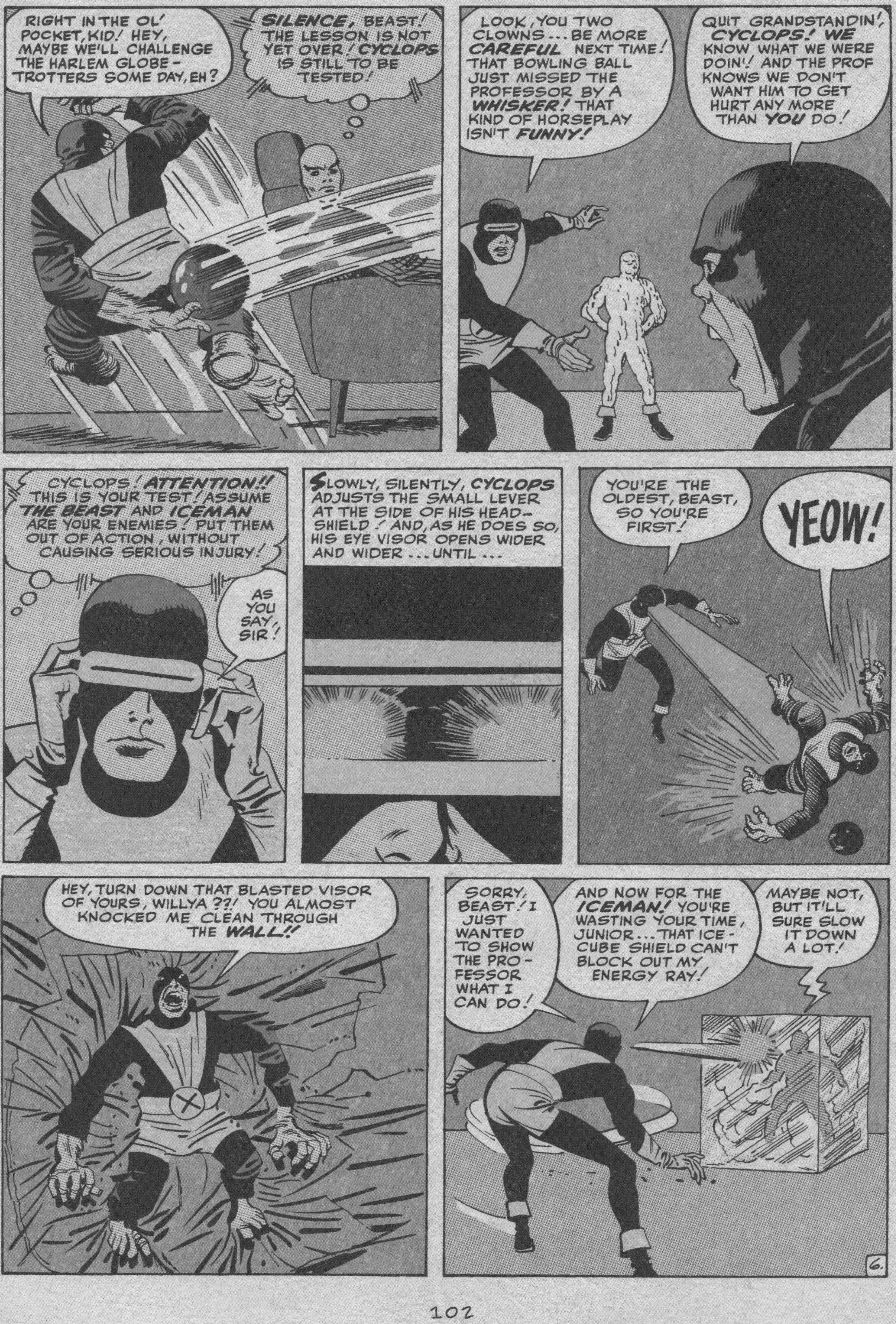

RIGHT IN THE OL' POCKET, KID! HEY, MAYBE WE'LL CHALLENGE THE HARLEM GLOBE-TROTTERS SOME DAY, EH?
SILENCE, BEAST! THE LESSON IS NOT YET OVER! CYCLOPS IS STILL TO BE TESTED!
LOOK, YOU TWO CLOWNS... BE MORE CAREFUL NEXT TIME! THAT BOWLING BALL JUST MISSED THE PROFESSOR BY A WHISKER! THAT KIND OF HORSEPLAY ISN'T FUNNY!
QUIT GRANDSTANDIN', CYCLOPS! WE KNOW WHAT WE WERE DOIN'! AND THE PROF KNOWS WE DON'T WANT HIM TO GET HURT ANY MORE THAN YOU DO!
CYCLOPS! ATTENTION!! THIS IS YOUR TEST! ASSUME THE BEAST AND ICEMAN ARE YOUR ENEMIES! PUT THEM OUT OF ACTION, WITHOUT CAUSING SERIOUS INJURY!
AS YOU SAY, SIR!
SLOWLY, SILENTLY, CYCLOPS ADJUSTS THE SMALL LEVER AT THE SIDE OF HIS HEAD-SHIELD! AND, AS HE DOES SO, HIS EYE VISOR OPENS WIDER AND WIDER... UNTIL...
YOU'RE THE OLDEST, BEAST, SO YOU'RE FIRST!
YEOW!
HEY, TURN DOWN THAT BLASTED VISOR OF YOURS, WILLYA??! YOU ALMOST KNOCKED ME CLEAN THROUGH THE WALL!!
SORRY, BEAST! I JUST WANTED TO SHOW THE PRO-FESSOR WHAT I CAN DO!
AND NOW FOR THE ICEMAN! YOU'RE WASTING YOUR TIME, JUNIOR... THAT ICE-CUBE SHIELD CAN'T BLOCK OUT MY ENERGY RAY!
MAYBE NOT, BUT IT'LL SURE SLOW IT DOWN A LOT!
6.

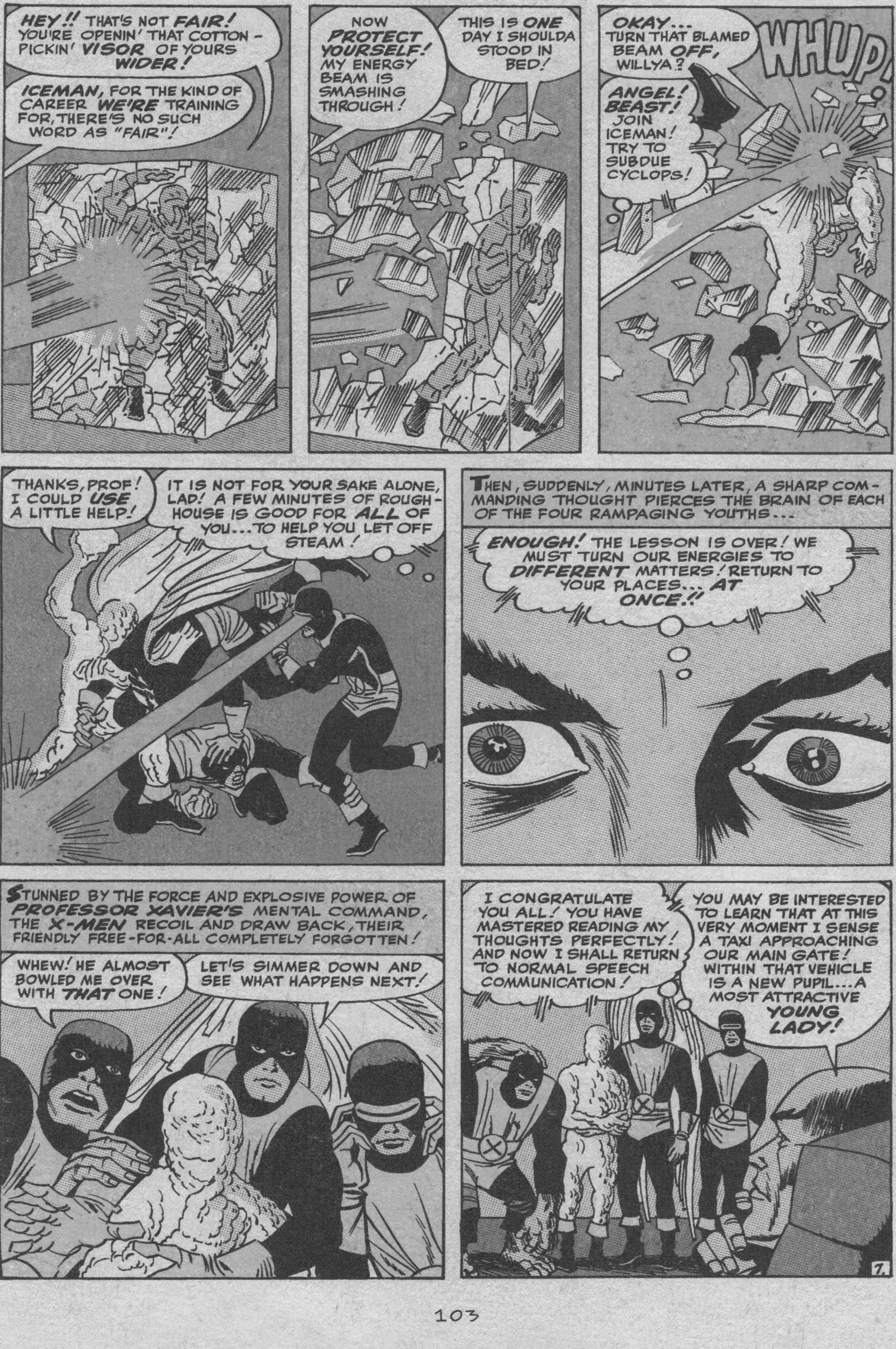
HEY!! THAT'S NOT FAIR! YOU'RE OPENIN' THAT COTTON-PICKIN' VISOR OF YOURS WIDER!
ICEMAN, FOR THE KIND OF CAREER WE'RE TRAINING FOR, THERE'S NO SUCH WORD AS "FAIR"!
NOW PROTECT YOURSELF! MY ENERGY BEAM IS SMASHING THROUGH!
THIS IS ONE DAY I SHOULDA STOOD IN BED!
OKAY... TURN THAT BLAMED BEAM OFF, WILLYA?
WHUP!
ANGEL! BEAST! JOIN ICEMAN! TRY TO SUBDUE CYCLOPS!
THANKS, PROF! I COULD USE A LITTLE HELP!
IT IS NOT FOR YOUR SAKE ALONE, LAD! A FEW MINUTES OF ROUGH-HOUSE IS GOOD FOR ALL OF YOU...TO HELP YOU LET OFF STEAM!
THEN, SUDDENLY, MINUTES LATER, A SHARP COMMANDING THOUGHT PIERCES THE BRAIN OF EACH OF THE FOUR RAMPAGING YOUTHS...
ENOUGH! THE LESSON IS OVER! WE MUST TURN OUR ENERGIES TO DIFFERENT MATTERS! RETURN TO YOUR PLACES... AT ONCE!!
STUNNED BY THE FORCE AND EXPLOSIVE POWER OF PROFESSOR XAVIER'S MENTAL COMMAND, THE X-MEN RECOIL AND DRAW BACK, THEIR FRIENDLY FREE-FOR-ALL COMPLETELY FORGOTTEN!
WHEW! HE ALMOST BOWLED ME OVER WITH THAT ONE!
LET'S SIMMER DOWN AND SEE WHAT HAPPENS NEXT!
I CONGRATULATE YOU ALL! YOU HAVE MASTERED READING MY THOUGHTS PERFECTLY! AND NOW I SHALL RETURN TO NORMAL SPEECH COMMUNICATION!
YOU MAY BE INTERESTED TO LEARN THAT AT THIS VERY MOMENT I SENSE A TAXI APPROACHING OUR MAIN GATE! WITHIN THAT VEHICLE IS A NEW PUPIL...A MOST ATTRACTIVE YOUNG LADY!
7.

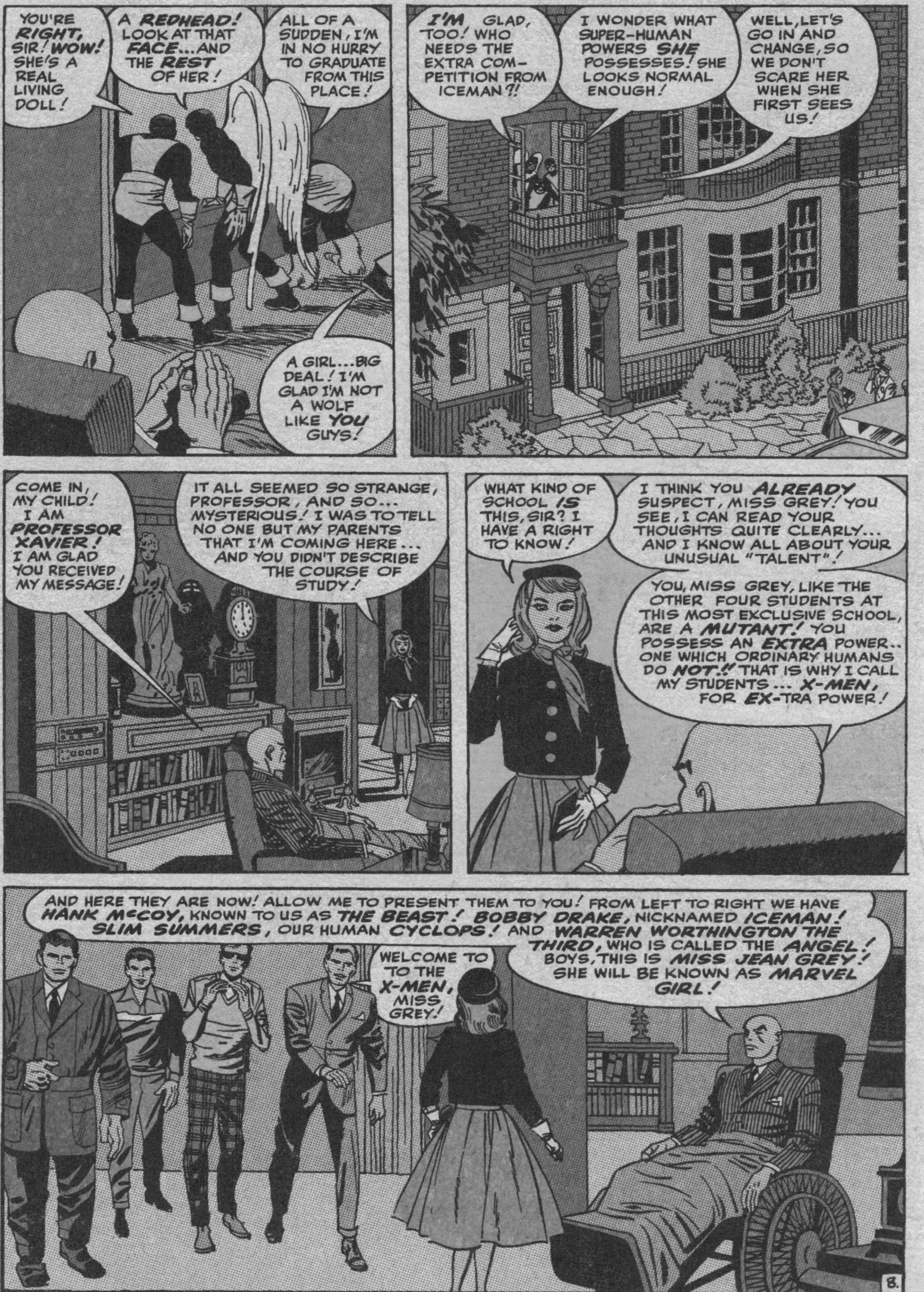
YOU'RE RIGHT, SIR! WOW! SHE'S A REAL LIVING DOLL!
A REDHEAD! LOOK AT THAT FACE...AND THE REST OF HER!
ALL OF A SUDDEN, I'M IN NO HURRY TO GRADUATE FROM THIS PLACE!
A GIRL...BIG DEAL! I'M GLAD I'M NOT A WOLF LIKE YOU GUYS!
I'M GLAD, TOO! WHO NEEDS THE EXTRA COMPETITION FROM ICEMAN?!
I WONDER WHAT SUPER-HUMAN POWERS SHE POSSESSES! SHE LOOKS NORMAL ENOUGH!
WELL, LET'S GO IN AND CHANGE, SO WE DON'T SCARE HER WHEN SHE FIRST SEES US!
COME IN, MY CHILD! I AM PROFESSOR XAVIER! I AM GLAD YOU RECEIVED MY MESSAGE!
IT ALL SEEMED SO STRANGE, PROFESSOR, AND SO... MYSTERIOUS! I WAS TO TELL NO ONE BUT MY PARENTS THAT I'M COMING HERE... AND YOU DIDN'T DESCRIBE THE COURSE OF STUDY!
WHAT KIND OF SCHOOL IS THIS, SIR? I HAVE A RIGHT TO KNOW!
I THINK YOU ALREADY SUSPECT, MISS GREY! YOU SEE, I CAN READ YOUR THOUGHTS QUITE CLEARLY... AND I KNOW ALL ABOUT YOUR UNUSUAL "TALENT"!
YOU, MISS GREY, LIKE THE OTHER FOUR STUDENTS AT THIS MOST EXCLUSIVE SCHOOL, ARE A MUTANT! YOU POSSESS AN EXTRA POWER.. ONE WHICH ORDINARY HUMANS DO NOT!! THAT IS WHY I CALL MY STUDENTS ... X-MEN, FOR EX-TRA POWER!
AND HERE THEY ARE NOW! ALLOW ME TO PRESENT THEM TO YOU! FROM LEFT TO RIGHT WE HAVE HANK McCOY, KNOWN TO US AS THE BEAST! BOBBY DRAKE, NICKNAMED ICEMAN! SLIM SUMMERS, OUR HUMAN CYCLOPS! AND WARREN WORTHINGTON THE THIRD, WHO IS CALLED THE ANGEL! BOYS, THIS IS MISS JEAN GREY! SHE WILL BE KNOWN AS MARVEL GIRL!
WELCOME TO TO THE X-MEN, MISS GREY!
8.

HOW COME HE'S CALLING YOU *MARVEL GIRL*, MISS GREY? WHAT POWER DO YOU HAVE?

SHE HAS *ONE* VERY OBVIOUS POWER...THE POWER TO MAKE A MAN'S *HEART* BEAT FASTER!

Y'KNOW SOMETHING, WARREN, IF I HAD *YOUR* LINE, I'D *SHOOT MYSELF!*

YOU'LL LEARN MORE ABOUT ME, BOYS, IN TIME!

WELL, NO TIME LIKE THE PRESENT! C'MON, SLIM, BRING THE LITTLE LADY A CHAIR!

HANK, I'D BRING HER THE WHOLE ROOM OF FURNITURE IF SHE ASKED ME!

THAT'S REALLY NOT NECESSARY, SLIM!

TH..THE CHAIR! IT SLID OUT OF MY HANDS!

Y!!!!!! HOLY SMOKE! WHAT'S GOIN' ON?!!

DON'T BE ALARMED, BOYS! I JUST THOUGHT I'D SAVE YOU THE TROUBLE!

ZZIPP

NOW, THEN, PROFESSOR, I BELIEVE WE CAN CONTINUE OUR INTERVIEW! AS YOU WERE SAYING...

I DON'T *GET* IT, SIR! WHAT HAPPENED TO THAT MOVING CHAIR??

PERHAPS YOU'D BETTER DEMONSTRATE A BIT *MORE*, JEAN!

VERY WELL, SIR! ALL MY LIFE I'VE HAD TO *CONCEAL* THIS POWER OF MINE...

NOW, I MUST ADMIT IT'S A PLEASURE TO BE ABLE TO PRACTICE *TELEPORTATION* OPENLY, WITHOUT FEAR OF BEING DISCOVERED! OBSERVE THAT BOOK!

BY THE POWER OF THOUGHT, I AM ABLE TO MOVE OBJECTS AT WILL!

BUT IT GETS BORING AFTER A WHILE, SO I'LL RETURN THE BOOK...LIKE THIS!

9.

THANK YOU, JEAN! AND NOW LET ME TELL YOU MORE ABOUT MY SCHOOL...

I WAS BORN OF PARENTS WHO HAD WORKED ON THE FIRST A-BOMB PROJECT! LIKE YOURSELVES, I AM A *MUTANT*... POSSIBLY THE *FIRST* SUCH MUTANT! I HAVE THE POWER TO READ MINDS, AND TO PROJECT MY OWN THOUGHTS INTO THE BRAINS OF OTHERS!

BUT, WHEN I WAS YOUNG, NORMAL PEOPLE FEARED ME, DISTRUSTED ME! I REALIZED THE HUMAN RACE IS NOT YET READY TO *ACCEPT* THOSE WITH EXTRA POWERS! SO I DECIDED TO BUILD A HAVEN... A SCHOOL FOR *X-MEN!*

HERE WE STAY, UNSUSPECTED BY NORMAL HUMANS, AS WE LEARN TO USE OUR POWERS FOR THE BENEFIT OF MANKIND... TO HELP THOSE WHO WOULD DISTRUST US IF THEY KNEW OF OUR EXISTENCE!

DUE TO A CHILDHOOD ACCIDENT, I MYSELF MUST REMAIN IN THIS CHAIR, BUT THROUGH A MASTER CONTROL PANEL I HAVE MANY DEVICES AT MY COMMAND... AND THROUGH MY *MIND*, I AM ALWAYS IN TOUCH WITH MY *X-MEN!*

AND NOW, I LEAVE YOU TO GET TO KNOW EACH OTHER BETTER!

LET ME BE THE FIRST TO WELCOME YOU TO THE *X-MEN*, BEAUTIFUL! MMMMM!

HANK! TAKE YOUR PAWS OFF HER!

OH!

FOR THE LUVVA PETE!

OH! *BOY!* WHAT A *GAL!* I HOPE SHE KEEPS THAT BIG APE UP THERE *FOREVER!*

DON'T WORRY, WARREN! I'M NOT EXACTLY *HELPLESS*, AS YOU CAN SEE!

HEY, C'MON! HAVE A HEART! I WAS ONLY TRYING TO BE *FRIENDLY!*

A FELLA COULD GET *DIZZY* UP HERE! LEMME DOWN, HUH? THIS IS *EMBARRASSING!*

VERY WELL, I'LL LET YOU DOWN!

THERE! YOU'RE DOWN!

OOOFF!!

WHUMP!

10.

I HOPE I WASN'T TOO ROUGH ON THE POOR DEAR!

NOT AT ALL, JEAN! WE DON'T USE KID GLOVES HERE! WE *HAVE* TO MAKE OUR TRAINING AS ROUGH AS POSSIBLE, TO PREPARE OUR- SELVES FOR OUR MISSION IN THE OUTSIDE WORLD!

THAT'S WHAT I'VE WANTED TO ASK! JUST WHAT EXACTLY *IS* OUR REAL MISSION, SIR?

JEAN, THERE ARE MANY MUTANTS WALK- ING THE EARTH... AND *MORE* ARE BORN EACH YEAR!

NOT *ALL* OF THEM WANT TO *HELP* MANKIND!...SOME *HATE* THE HUMAN RACE, AND WISH TO *DESTROY* IT! SOME FEEL THAT THE MUTANTS SHOULD BE THE REAL RULERS OF EARTH! IT IS OUR JOB TO PROTECT MANKIND FROM THOSE... FROM THE *EVIL MUTANTS!*

AT THAT VERY MOMENT, JUST SUCH A MUTANT PREPARES TO *STRIKE*... IN A SECRET LABORA- TORY NEAR CAPE CITADEL!

THE MOMENT IS AT HAND!

ALL MY MONTHS OF PREPARATION AND PLANNING SHALL NOW PAY OFF!

THE HUMAN RACE NO LONGER DESERVES DOMINION OVER THE PLANET EARTH! THE DAY OF THE *MUTANTS* IS UPON US!

THE FIRST PHASE OF MY PLAN SHALL BE TO SHOW MY POWER...TO MAKE HOMO SAPIENS BOW TO HOMO *SUPERIOR!*

THE MIGHTIEST ROCKET OF ALL IS ABOUT TO BE LAUNCHED! USING MAXIMUM SECURITY PRECAUTIONS, THE GOVERNMENT FEELS *NOTHING* CAN PREVENT ITS SUCCESSFUL FLIGHT!

BUT HERE, MILES FROM THE LAUNCH- ING SITE, I, THE MIRACULOUS *MAGNETO*, ALONE SHALL MAKE A MOCKERY OF THEIR GREATEST EFFORT!

11.

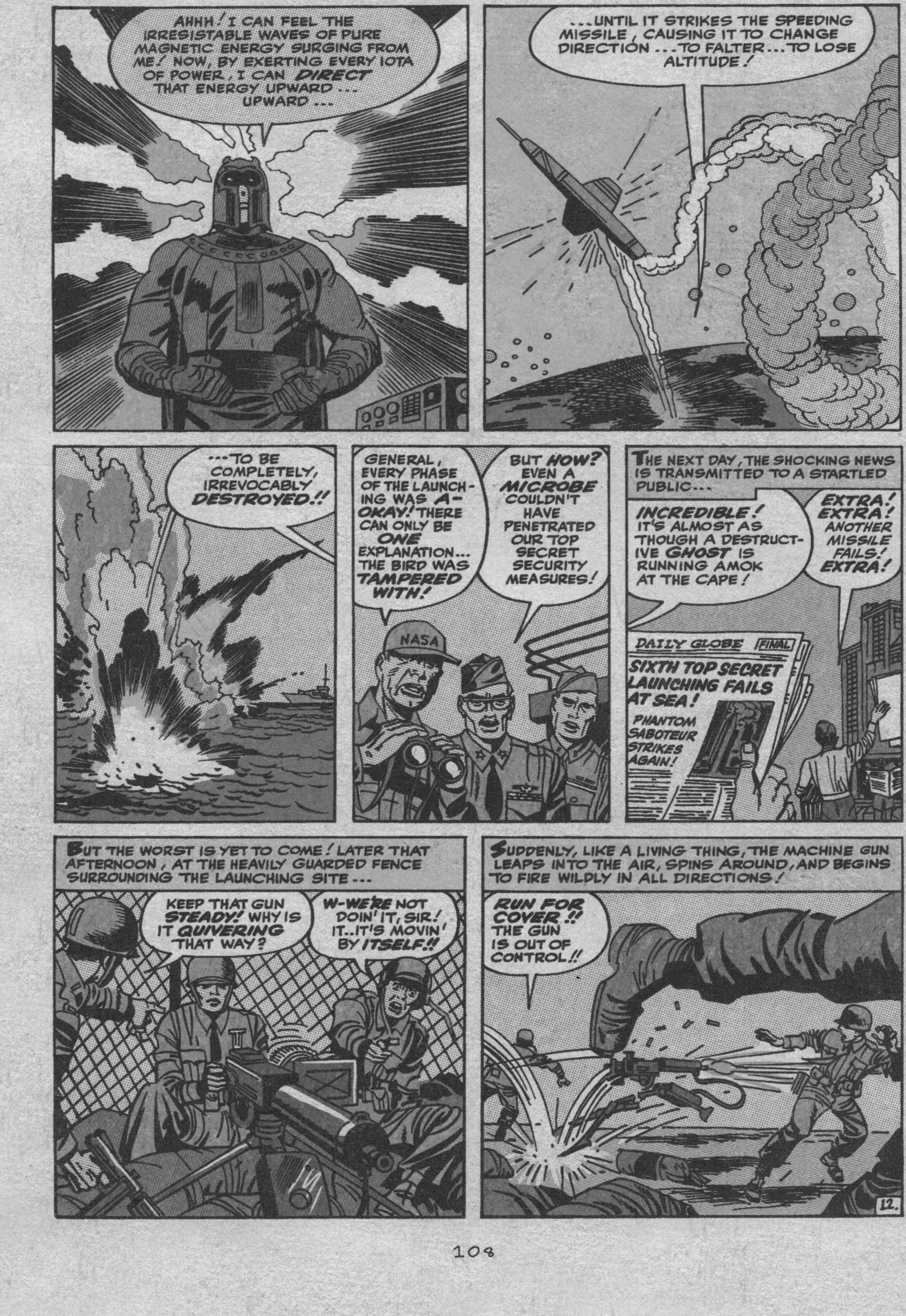
AHHH! I CAN FEEL THE IRRESISTABLE WAVES OF PURE MAGNETIC ENERGY SURGING FROM ME! NOW, BY EXERTING EVERY IOTA OF POWER, I CAN DIRECT THAT ENERGY UPWARD --- UPWARD ---
...UNTIL IT STRIKES THE SPEEDING MISSILE, CAUSING IT TO CHANGE DIRECTION ... TO FALTER ... TO LOSE ALTITUDE!
---TO BE COMPLETELY, IRREVOCABLY DESTROYED.!!
GENERAL, EVERY PHASE OF THE LAUNCHING WAS A-OKAY! THERE CAN ONLY BE ONE EXPLANATION... THE BIRD WAS TAMPERED WITH!
BUT HOW? EVEN A MICROBE COULDN'T HAVE PENETRATED OUR TOP SECRET SECURITY MEASURES!
NASA
THE NEXT DAY, THE SHOCKING NEWS IS TRANSMITTED TO A STARTLED PUBLIC...
INCREDIBLE! IT'S ALMOST AS THOUGH A DESTRUCTIVE GHOST IS RUNNING AMOK AT THE CAPE!
EXTRA! EXTRA! ANOTHER MISSILE FAILS! EXTRA!
DAILY GLOBE FINAL
SIXTH TOP SECRET LAUNCHING FAILS AT SEA!
PHANTOM SABOTEUR STRIKES AGAIN!
BUT THE WORST IS YET TO COME! LATER THAT AFTERNOON, AT THE HEAVILY GUARDED FENCE SURROUNDING THE LAUNCHING SITE ---
KEEP THAT GUN STEADY! WHY IS IT QUIVERING THAT WAY?
W-WE'RE NOT DOIN' IT, SIR! IT..IT'S MOVIN' BY ITSELF!!
SUDDENLY, LIKE A LIVING THING, THE MACHINE GUN LEAPS INTO THE AIR, SPINS AROUND, AND BEGINS TO FIRE WILDLY IN ALL DIRECTIONS!
RUN FOR COVER!! THE GUN IS OUT OF CONTROL!!
12.

BUT, THE MACHINE GUN IS NOT THE *ONLY* THING THAT SUDDENLY, MADDENINGLY SEEM TO GO AMOK!

RUN! THE TANK IS MOVING BY *ITSELF!* GANGWAY!

IT..IT'S *IMPOSSIBLE!* AND YET... IT'S ACTING LIKE IT HAS A MIND OF ITS OWN! LIKE IT'S *TRYING* TO MENACE US!

SWISH!

CLANK!

CLANK!

WITHIN SECONDS, THE ENTIRE INSTALLATION IS ALARMED, AS EMERGENCY MEASURES ARE SWIFTLY BROUGHT INTO PLAY! AND THEN...

SOUND THE ALARM! *CONDITION RED!* ALERT THE PENTAGON!

GENERAL! *LOOK!* ABOVE US... IN THE SKY!

APPEARING AS THOUGH BY MAGIC, OVER THE HEADS OF THE ASTONISHED TROOPS, HUGE LETTERS TAKE SHAPE... COMPOSED OF THE DUST PARTICLES FROM THE AIR ITSELF, SKILLFULLY MAGNETIZED INTO A MESSAGE BY THE UNSEEN MUTANT!

SURRENDER THE BASE OR I'LL TAKE IT BY FORCE!

Magneto

MAGNETO? WHO... *WHAT* IS MAGNETO??

GENERAL, WHAT DOES IT *MEAN?* IS SOMEONE PLAYING A GRIM *PRANK?*

YOU SAW THAT MACHINE GUN... THAT TANK... RAMPAGING OUT OF CONTROL! THIS IS *NO JOKE,* COLONEL!

THEY ARE STARTLED! *GOOD!* THE ELEMENT OF SURPRISE IS IN MY FAVOR!

BUT THEY'RE MAKING NO MOVE TO SURRENDER! PERHAPS THEY NEED *ANOTHER* DEMONSTRATION OF MY POWER!

I'LL DIRECT MY MAGNETIC IMPULSES INTO THIS ENERGIZER, TO INCREASE THEIR POWER, AND THEN I'LL LEAVE THE HELPLESS HOMO SAPIENS WITH NO ROOM FOR DOUBT!

13.

AN INSTANT LATER, INVISIBLE WAVES OF PURE, POWERFUL MAGNETIC ENERGY FLOW IRRESISTIBLY INTO AN UNDERGROUND SILO WHERE ONE OF DEMOCRACY'S SILENT SENTINELS WAIT, AT THE READY!

AND THEN, MANIPULATED BY A SINISTER INTELLIGENCE, MANY HUNDREDS OF YARDS AWAY, THE MAGNETIC FORCE LIFTS THE SILO HEAD, ACTIVATING THE MIGHTY MISSILE!!

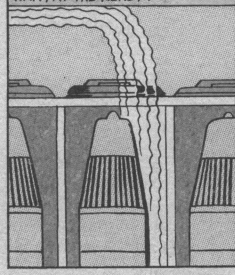  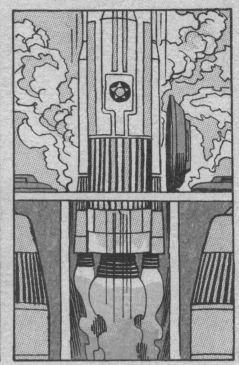

DEMONSTRATING A POWER WHICH THE HUMAN BRAIN IS ALMOST UNABLE TO COMPREHEND, *MAGNETO* CAUSES THE GRIM ROCKET TO FALL INTO THE SEA MANY MILES FROM SHORE, NEXT TO AN UNMANNED TARGET SHIP!

BUT *STILL*, THE THOUGHT OF SURRENDER NEVER CROSSES THE MINDS OF THE FIGHTING-MAD BASE PERSONNEL!

SERGEANT! ORDER THE GUARD *DOUBLED* AT EVERY MISSILE CONTROL CENTER! ANY ROCKET DEEMED A MENACE IS TO BE DESTROYED *INSTANTLY!*

SOME POWER BEYOND OUR UNDERSTANDING IS AFFECTING OUR WEAPONS! WE MUST *FIND* THIS *MAGNETO!*

GENERAL, *LOOK!* THAT COMMOTION AT THE MAIN GATE! IT SEEMS THAT *HE* HAS FOUND *US* FIRST!

HOLD IT, MAC! IF YOU'RE LOOKIN' FOR A *MASQUERADE PARTY*, YOU'VE COME TO THE WRONG PLACE! BEAT IT!

WELL SAID, GUARD! WHAT A PITY YOU HAVE NO *POWER* TO BACK UP SUCH IMPRESSIVE WORDS! YOUR PUNY WEAPONS CANNOT STOP *ME!*

THEY *CAN'T*, EH? ONE LITTLE BURST OVER YOUR HEAD WILL SURELY CHANGE YOUR MIND!

HEY! WHA-WHAT GIVES? THE GUN WON'T *FIRE!* THE TRIGGER SEEMS LOCKED IN PLACE!

I CAN'T EVEN *LIFT* MY GUN! FEELS LIKE IT WEIGHS A *TON!*

14.

NOW I'LL MERELY ALTER MY MAGNETIC WAVES FROM POSITIVE TO *NEGATIVE*, SO THAT THEY WILL *REPEL* ANYTHING THAT COMES WITHIN RANGE! *NOTHING* CAN TOUCH ME AS I WALK TO MY OBJECTIVE!

WE CAN'T *STOP* HIM! CALL FOR RE-INFORCEMENTS!

I'M 'WAY *AHEAD* OF YA, PAL!

BUT, THE ADDITIONAL REINFORCEMENTS ARE EQUALLY POWERLESS TO STOP THE ONE-MAN INVASION OF THE STRATEGIC BASE!

IT..IT'S LIKE HE'S GOT AN INVISIBLE *BARRIER* 'ROUND HIM, HURLING US AWAY!

THERE! BY SIMPLY NARROWING MY MAGNETIC WAVES ALL AROUND THE LESSER HUMANS, I CAN KEEP THEM CONFINED TO THAT AREA UNTIL I REACH THEIR OFFICER-IN-COMMAND!

AND FINALLY...

HOLD IT, MEN! ALL RIGHT, WHO-EVER YOU ARE...IF YOU'VE SOMETHING TO SAY, YOU'VE GOT SIXTY SECONDS TO SAY IT!

WRONG, GENERAL! I HAVE ALL THE TIME IN THE WORLD! AND NOW, I, THE MIRACULOUS *MAGNETO*, CLAIM THIS ENTIRE INSTAL-LATION...IN THE NAME OF *HOMO SUPERIOR!!*

THAT *DOES* IT! *TAKE HIM*, MEN! WE'LL SHOW HIM THAT...

WHA...WHAT'S *THAT??* WE CAN'T MOVE OUT OF THIS SMALL AREA! IT'S LIKE BEING ENCIRCLED BY AN INVISIBLE, LIVING *FENCE!*

THAT "LIVING FENCE" AS YOU CALL IT, IS THE SYMBOL OF MY GREAT POWER! IT IS A MIGHTY SHIELD OF *MAGNETIC ENERGY!*

AND SO I HAVE NOW ACCOMPLISHED MY FIRST OBJECTIVE! GENTLEMEN, CAPE CITADEL IS *MINE!*

15.

MEANWHILE, IN A DORMITORY ROOM AT THE WORLD'S MOST EXCLUSIVE PRIVATE SCHOOL, JEAN GREY IS ABSORBED WITH HER REFLECTION IN THE FULL-LENGTH MIRROR...THE REFLECTION WHICH REVEALS THE NEW *MARVEL GIRL!*

MMM, WHOEVER DESIGNED THIS UNIFORM COULD HAVE GIVEN CHRISTIAN DIOR A RUN FOR HIS MONEY!

WHERE DID THE NEW DOLL GO? OH... *THERE* SHE IS!

WOWEE! LOOKS LIKE SHE WAS *POURED* INTO THAT UNIFORM!

YOU AGAIN! *HONESTLY!* CAN'T A GIRL HAVE ANY *PRIVACY* AROUND HERE?

EASY, GORGEOUS! WE WERE JUST PASSIN' BY! DON'T GO GETTIN' *MAD!*

SUDDENLY, THE YOUNGSTERS' BANTERING IS FORGOTTEN AS A SHARP COMMANDING *THOUGHT* REGISTERS IN THE BRAIN OF EACH OF THEM!

ATTENTION, X-MEN! THIS IS PROFESSOR XAVIER! REPORT TO MY STUDY IMMEDIATELY... YOU HAVE FIFTEEN SECONDS! NO EXCUSES WILL BE TOLERATED!

WOW! DID ALL OF YOU RECEIVE THAT MENTAL BLAST?

AND *HOW!* IT SOUNDED LIKE A TRUMPET'S BLARE! *LET'S GO!*

EXACTLY FIFTEEN SECONDS LATER...

I COMMEND YOU FOR YOUR PUNCTUALITY!

YOU'RE SPEAKING *ALOUD!* THAT MEANS IT'S IMPORTANT!

I HAVE JUST HEARD A BULLETIN ON THE RADIO WHICH CONCERNS YOU!

I NEVER SAW THE PROFESSOR LIKE THIS BEFORE ...SO GRIM, SO INTENSE!

A CRISIS HAS OCCURRED AT CAPE CITADEL WHICH LEADS ME TO BELIEVE THE FIRST OF THE EVIL MUTANTS HAS MADE HIS APPEARANCE! THIS WILL BE YOUR BAPTISM OF FIRE! YOU ARE TO GO TO THE CAPE...AND *DEFEAT HIM!*

YAYBO!! ACTION AT LAST! *GANGWAY!*

CAPE CITADEL! WHATEVER THE MENACE IS, IT MUST INVOLVE OUR *MISSILES!*

WONDER WHO THE MUTANT *BADDIE* IS?

HAH! I CAN GET READY FASTER THAN THE REST OF YOU! ALL I HAVETA DO IS ICE UP AND PUT ON MY BOOTS!

16

AS FOR ME, IT'LL BE A PLEASURE TO GET OUT OF THIS HARNESS I HAVE TO WEAR!

HAVING A PAIR OF WINGS CAN BE MORE TROUBLE THAN YOU'D GUESS!

THESE RESTRAINING BELTS OF MINE KEEP MY WINGS FROM BULGING UNDER MY SUIT, BUT AFTER A WHILE THEY FEEL LIKE I'M WEARING A STRAIT-JACKET!

AHHH! THAT'S MORE LIKE IT! NOW I FEEL LIKE MYSELF AGAIN! NOW THE ANGEL IS READY TO SPREAD HIS WINGS ..AND FLY!

BUT THE TIME HAS NOT YET COME FOR THE ANGEL TO FLY! INSTEAD, THE BAND OF SUPER-HUMAN TEEN-AGERS ARE DRIVEN TO THE AIRPORT IN PROFESSOR XAVIER'S SPECIALLY-BUILT ROLLS ROYCE, WITH ITS DARK-TINTED WINDOWS!

BOY! IT MUSTA TAKEN A HEAP OF GREEN STAMPS TO BY A CHARIOT LIKE THIS!

NO JOKING, PLEASE! CONCENTRATE ON YOUR MISSION! REVIEW YOUR POWERS! YOUR FOE IS CERTAIN TO BE HIGHLY DANGEROUS!

MINUTES LATER, IN THE PROFESSOR'S REMOTE-CONTROL PRIVATE JET, THE X-MEN AND MARVEL GIRL ARE WINGING TOWARDS CAPE CITADEL AT NEARLY THE SPEED OF SOUND!

YOU MEAN THE PROFESSOR IS GUIDING THIS PLANE FROM THE GROUND... BY THOUGHT IMPULSES?! IT'S UN-BELIEVABLE!

LOOK, DOLL... WHEN YOU JOIN THE X-MEN, YOU REALIZE NOTHING'S UN-BELIEVABLE!

A SHORT TIME LATER, AT THE CAPE!...

CEASE FIRING! IT'S USELESS! WE HAVEN'T ANYTHING IN OUR ARSENAL THAT'LL PENETRATE MAGNETO'S MAGNETIC FORCE FIELD!

TO ALL INTENTS AND PURPOSES, HE'S IN FULL CONTROL OF THE INSTALLATION, WHILE WE'RE ON THE OUTSIDE, LOOKING IN!

WITH DUE RESPECT, GENERAL, I REPRESENT THE X-MEN! PERHAPS WE CAN HELP!

X-MEN?! WHAT THE..?!

17.

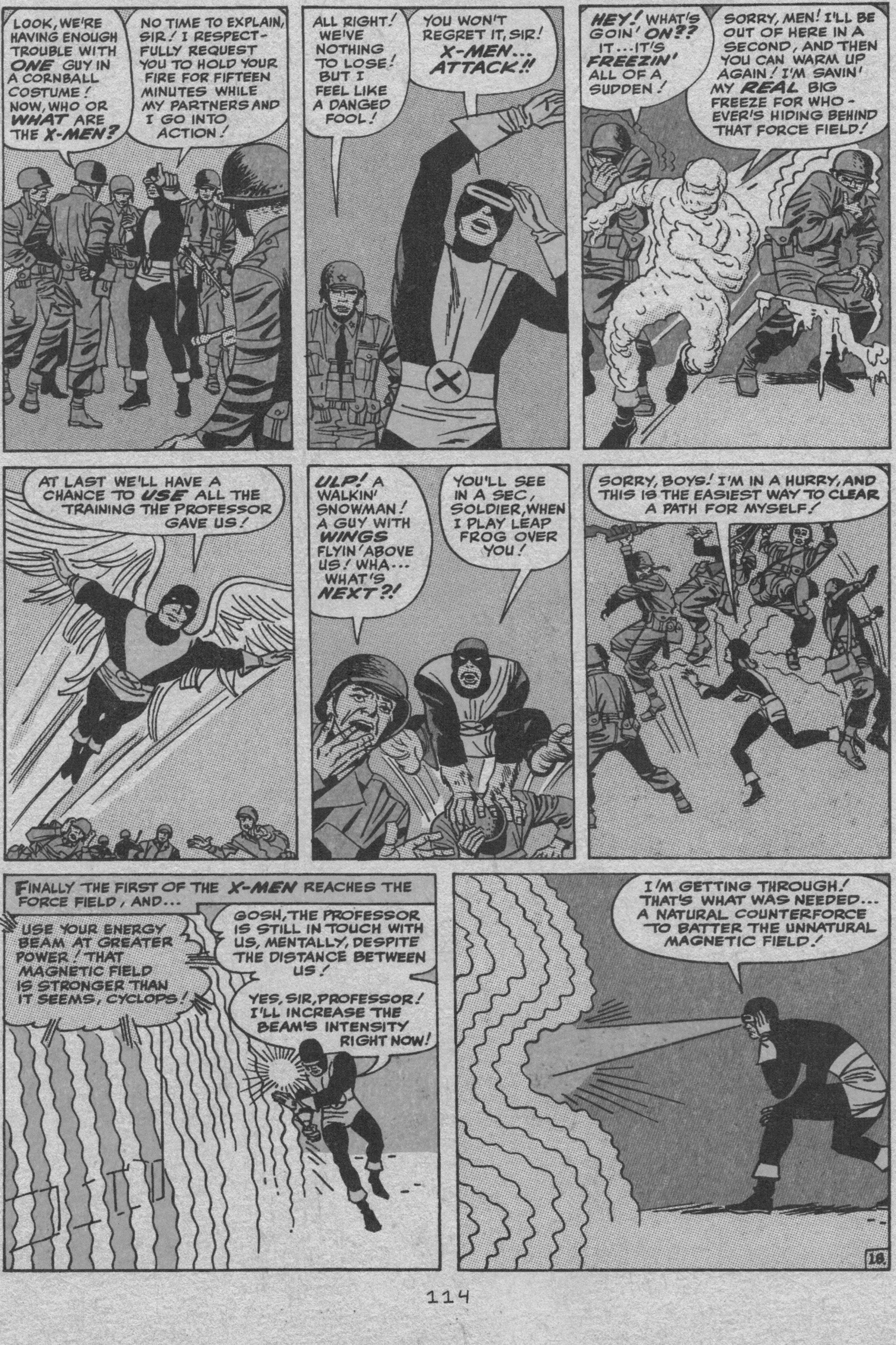

LOOK, WE'RE HAVING ENOUGH TROUBLE WITH ONE GUY IN A CORNBALL COSTUME! NOW, WHO OR WHAT ARE THE X-MEN?
NO TIME TO EXPLAIN, SIR! I RESPECTFULLY REQUEST YOU TO HOLD YOUR FIRE FOR FIFTEEN MINUTES WHILE MY PARTNERS AND I GO INTO ACTION!
ALL RIGHT! WE'VE NOTHING TO LOSE! BUT I FEEL LIKE A DANGED FOOL!
YOU WON'T REGRET IT, SIR! X-MEN... ATTACK!!
HEY! WHAT'S GOIN' ON?? IT...IT'S FREEZIN' ALL OF A SUDDEN!
SORRY, MEN! I'LL BE OUT OF HERE IN A SECOND, AND THEN YOU CAN WARM UP AGAIN! I'M SAVIN' MY REAL BIG FREEZE FOR WHO-EVER'S HIDING BEHIND THAT FORCE FIELD!
AT LAST WE'LL HAVE A CHANCE TO USE ALL THE TRAINING THE PROFESSOR GAVE US!
ULP! A WALKIN' SNOWMAN! A GUY WITH WINGS FLYIN' ABOVE US! WHA... WHAT'S NEXT?!
YOU'LL SEE IN A SEC, SOLDIER, WHEN I PLAY LEAP FROG OVER YOU!
SORRY, BOYS! I'M IN A HURRY, AND THIS IS THE EASIEST WAY TO CLEAR A PATH FOR MYSELF!
FINALLY THE FIRST OF THE X-MEN REACHES THE FORCE FIELD, AND...
USE YOUR ENERGY BEAM AT GREATER POWER! THAT MAGNETIC FIELD IS STRONGER THAN IT SEEMS, CYCLOPS!
GOSH, THE PROFESSOR IS STILL IN TOUCH WITH US, MENTALLY, DESPITE THE DISTANCE BETWEEN US!
YES, SIR, PROFESSOR! I'LL INCREASE THE BEAM'S INTENSITY RIGHT NOW!
I'M GETTING THROUGH! THAT'S WHAT WAS NEEDED... A NATURAL COUNTERFORCE TO BATTER THE UNNATURAL MAGNETIC FIELD!
18

AND NOW, I'LL SWITCH TO *MAXIMUM POWER*! I CAN ONLY MAINTAIN THIS PRESSURE FOR A FEW SECONDS, BUT... *AHH!* I *DID* IT!

BEHIND THE FORCE FIELD, THE NATURAL ENERGY FEED-BACK WEAKENS THE STARTLED *MAGNETO!*

SOME POWER IS ATTACKING ME! SOME POWER AS SUPER-HUMAN AS MY *OWN!*

I WAS STAGGERED BECAUSE I WAS UN-PREPARED FOR ANY SUCH ONSLAUGHT! BUT NOW THAT I'M FOREWARNED, I CAN DEFEAT *ANY* FOE...NO MATTER *HOW* SUPER-HUMAN HE MAY BE!

BUT MAGNETO IS SOON TO LEARN THAT HE HAS MORE THAN ONE FOE TO CONTEND WITH! HE HAS THE FIGHTING BAND OF *X-MEN!*

CYCLOPS ALMOST KNOCKED HIM-SELF OUT, BUT HE GOT US *IN* HERE! NOW LET'S PROVE WE CAN CARRY THE BALL!

LOOK SHARP, *X-MEN!* YOU ARE FACING A DANGER-OUS ENEMY!

AHHH! NOW I SEE MY ANTAGONISTS! FIVE COSTUMED YOUTHS! SURELY ALL THEIR POWERS PUT TOGETHER CAN BE NO MATCH FOR *MINE!*

BUT I WILL LET THE BASE'S *HUNTER MISSILES* DO MY FIGHTING FOR ME! THEY WILL HUNT THE FIVE DOWN, ATTRACTED BY THEIR BODY HEAT!

INTERCEPTOR MISSILES

FIRE

AND SO, AT THE PRESS OF A BUTTON, *MAGNETO* UNLEASHES FIVE OF THE MOST SOPHISTICATED WEAPONS EVER CREATED...ALL ZEROED IN ON THE *X-MEN!*

19.

THE FIRST TARGET FOR THE MERCILESS MISSILES IS THE *ANGEL*, FLYING CLOSEST TO THEM!

GOT TO *DODGE* THEM, SOMEHOW!

IT'S NO USE! THEY'RE TOO *FAST!* GAINING ON ME....!

HANG ON, ANGEL! I CAN HELP YOU...WHILE THEY'RE STILL WITHIN RANGE!

THESE *ICE GRENADES* MUSTN'T MISS! THEY'RE THE ANGEL'S ONLY CHANCE!

JUST AS THE HUNTER MISSILES ARE ATTRACTED BY HEAT, SO ARE THE ICEMAN'S ICE GRENADES ATTRACTED BY THE MISSILES' SPEED, AND SO...

BULL'S EYE!

IT *WORKED!* THE ICE COVERED THEIR NOSES, PREVENTING 'EM FROM EXPLODING! NOW, WITH THEIR GUIDANCE SYSTEMS KNOCKED OUT, THEY'VE GOT TO DROP TO THE GROUND!

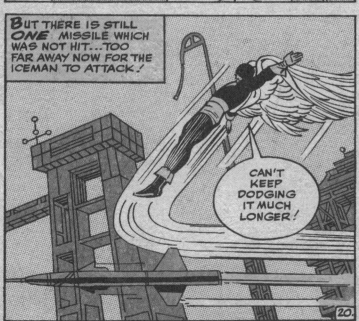

BUT THERE IS STILL *ONE* MISSILE WHICH WAS NOT HIT...TOO FAR AWAY NOW FOR THE ICEMAN TO ATTACK!

CAN'T KEEP DODGING IT MUCH LONGER!

20.

ANGEL! LOWER... FLY LOWER! COME TOWARDS ME! HURRY!

OKAY, BEAST! BUT WHAT...??

JUST WAIT AND SEE, PAL!

HAH! GOT IT!

GOOD WORK, BEAST! NOW RELEASE IT! I'LL TAKE OVER NOW!

AND THEN, USING HER AMAZING TELEKINETIC POWER, MARVEL GIRL MENTALLY HURLS THE MISSILE INTO THE SEA, WHERE IT HARMLESSLY DETONATES UPON IMPACT!

DESPITE THEIR SEEMING YOUTH AND INEXPERIENCE, THEY ARE MIGHTY ANTAGONISTS! I MUST NEVER AGAIN MAKE THE MISTAKE OF UNDER-ESTIMATING THEM! BUT I SHALL STILL PROVE TO BE THEIR MASTER!

THERE HE IS! I'VE FOUND HIM!! X-MEN, ATTACK!!

WRONG, YOU FLYING FOOL! IT IS I, MAGNETO, WHO HAVE FOUND YOU!

SEE HOW EASILY I CAN STOP YOUR FLIGHT BY MAGNETICALLY HURLING EVERY NEARBY OBJECT WHICH IS NOT BOLTED DOWN!

21.

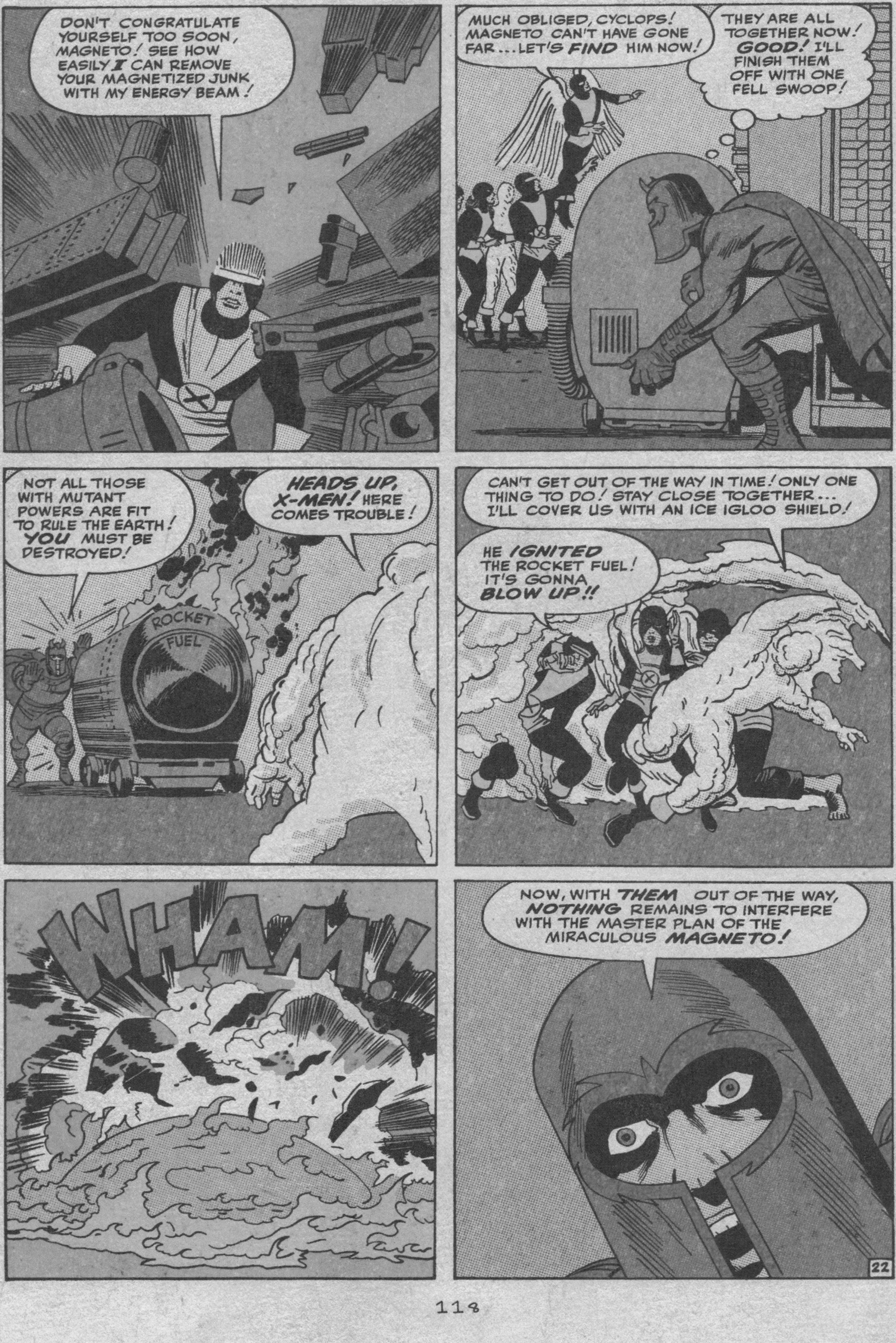
DON'T CONGRATULATE YOURSELF TOO SOON, MAGNETO! SEE HOW EASILY I CAN REMOVE YOUR MAGNETIZED JUNK WITH MY ENERGY BEAM!
MUCH OBLIGED, CYCLOPS! MAGNETO CAN'T HAVE GONE FAR... LET'S FIND HIM NOW!
THEY ARE ALL TOGETHER NOW! GOOD! I'LL FINISH THEM OFF WITH ONE FELL SWOOP!
NOT ALL THOSE WITH MUTANT POWERS ARE FIT TO RULE THE EARTH! YOU MUST BE DESTROYED!
HEADS UP, X-MEN! HERE COMES TROUBLE!
ROCKET FUEL
CAN'T GET OUT OF THE WAY IN TIME! ONLY ONE THING TO DO! STAY CLOSE TOGETHER... I'LL COVER US WITH AN ICE IGLOO SHIELD!
HE IGNITED THE ROCKET FUEL! IT'S GONNA BLOW UP!!
WHAM!
NOW, WITH THEM OUT OF THE WAY, NOTHING REMAINS TO INTERFERE WITH THE MASTER PLAN OF THE MIRACULOUS MAGNETO!
22

THE HEAT IS SO INTENSE THAT EVEN *I* CANNOT GET CLOSE TO IT! I MUST WALK CAREFULLY AROUND IT!

THAT *BEAM*... FROM BENEATH THE GROUND!! WHAT... WHAT DOES IT *MEAN*?

IT MEANS YOUR *FINISH*, MAGNETO!

CYCLOPS CREATED A TUNNEL FOR US UNDER THE BLAST WITH HIS ENERGY BEAM... SAVING US FROM THE IMPACT! AND *NOW*...

YOU HAVEN'T DEFEATED ME *YET*! I CAN STILL ESCAPE YOU, FLYING BY MEANS OF MAGNETIC REPULSION!

UGH! HE CREATED ANOTHER MAGNETIC FORCE FIELD! CAN'T FLY THROUGH!

DON'T WORRY, ANGEL! WE'LL BREACH IT IN NO TIME!

AND BREACH IT THEY DO! BUT BY THAT TIME...

HE'S *GONE*! BUT WHERE...?

A MUTANT WITH *HIS* POWERS? HE COULD BE *ANY-WHERE*! BUT AT LEAST WE'VE BEATEN HIM FOR *NOW*!

YOUR BASE IS OPERATIONAL AGAIN, GENERAL! MAGNETO IS GONE!

UNCANNY! YOUR FIFTEEN MINUTES ARE NOT YET UP!

YOU CALL YOURSELVES THE *X-MEN*! I WILL NOT ASK YOU TO REVEAL YOUR TRUE IDENTITIES, BUT I PROMISE YOU THAT BEFORE THIS DAY IS OVER, THE NAME X-MEN WILL BE THE MOST HONORED IN MY COMMAND!

THANK YOU, SIR! AND SHOULD AMERICA'S SECURITY EVER AGAIN BE THREAT-ENED, THE X-MEN WILL BE BACK!

WELL DONE, STUDENTS! YOU HAVE JUSTIFIED ALL OUR LONG HOURS OF TRAINING... ALL OUR SACRIFICES... ALL OUR DREAMS! AND NOW, RETURN TO ME, MY *X-MEN*!

23.

YOU HAVE JUST FINISHED THE NEWEST, MOST UNUSUAL TALE IN THE ANNALS OF MODERN MAGAZINES! BUT THE BEST IS YET TO COME! FOR FANTASY AT ITS GREATEST, DON'T MISS ISSUE #2 OF X-MEN, THE STRANGEST SUPER-HEROES OF ALL!

ABOUT THE AUTHOR

PHOTO BY AUDRA WIST, USED WITH PERMISSION

ED PISKOR (1982- INSERT DATE HERE) IS A GENETIC **MUTANT** WHO MAKES COMICS IN THE SMALL TOWN OF **PITTSBURGH, PA.** HE STARTED OUT DRAWING **AMERICAN SPLENDOR** COMICS FOR **HARVEY PEKAR**. **WIZZYWIG** (TOP SHELF, 2012) WAS HIS FIRST SOLO EFFORT. HIS **HIP HOP FAMILY TREE** SERIES (FANTA-GRAPHICS, 2013- PRESENT) IS THE ONE THAT GOT HIM AN **EISNER** AWARD AND A SPOT ON THE **NEW YORK TIMES BEST-SELLERS** LIST FOR A WEEK.

PISKOR IS DEBATING WHETHER OR NOT HE SHOULD REVEAL HIS GENETIC MUTATION IN A FUTURE VOLUME OF **X-MEN: GRAND DESIGN**.

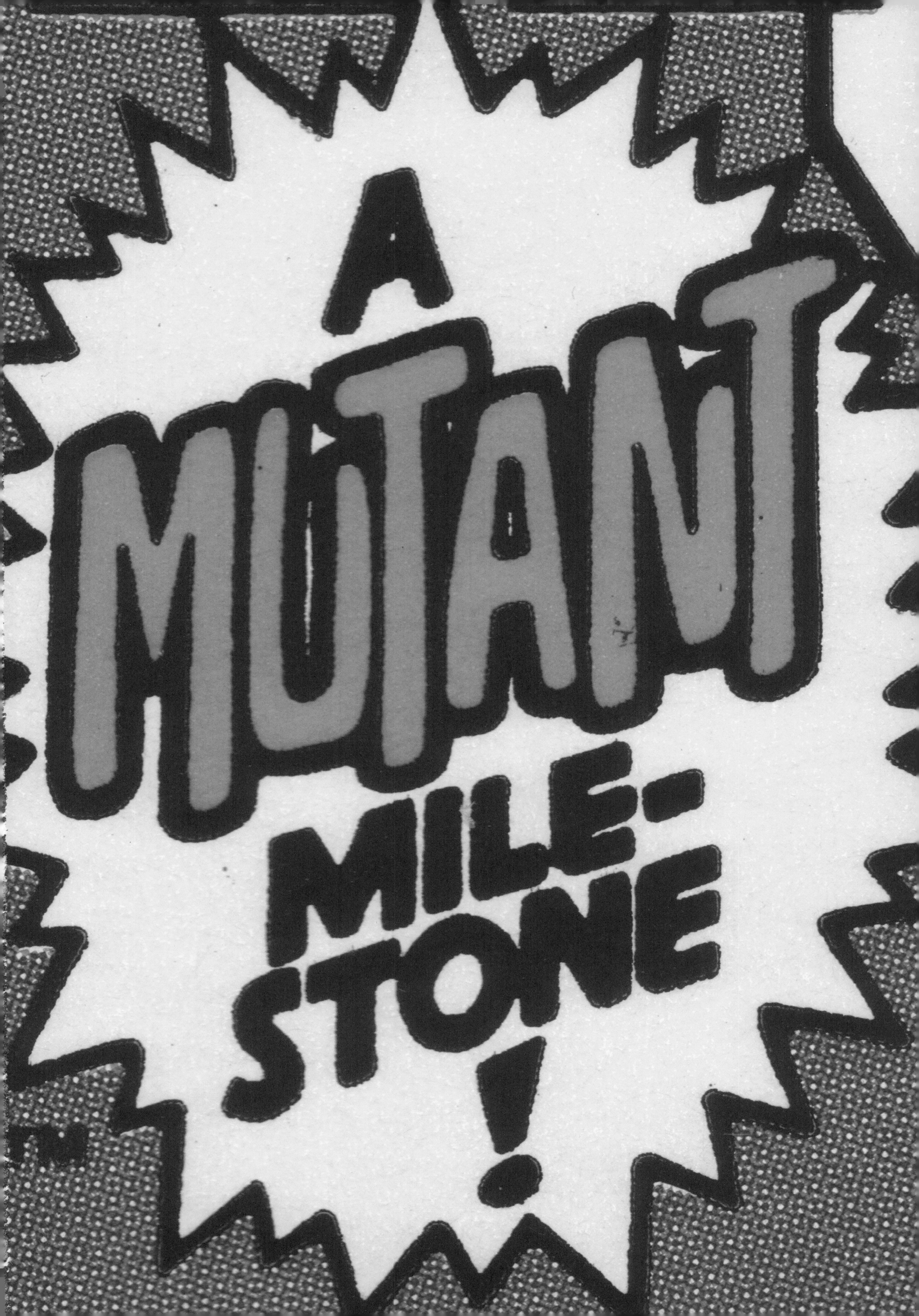
A MUTANT MILE-STONE!

MARVEL
COMICS
GROUP 12¢

MARVEL
COMICS 12¢
GROUP

MARVEL
COMICS
GROUP
12¢ IND. 32 MAY

30¢ CC 101 OCT 02461

MARVEL® ©1984 MARVEL COMICS GROUP
60¢ 181 MAY CC 02461
APPROVED BY THE COMICS CODE AUTHORITY

MARVEL® ©1983
60¢ 189 JAN CC 02461
APPROVED BY THE COMICS CODE AUTHORITY

MARVEL® ©1984 MARVEL COMICS GROUP
60¢ 190 FEB 02461
APPROVED BY THE COMICS CODE AUTHORITY

MARVEL® ©1985 MARVEL COMICS GROUP
65¢ 198 OCT CC 02461
APPROVED BY THE COMICS CODE AUTHORITY

MARVEL® ©1985 MARVEL COMICS GROUP
$1.25 200 DEC CC 02461
APPROVED BY THE COMICS CODE AUTHORITY

MARVEL® ©1988 MARVEL ENT. GROUP, INC.
$1.00 US $1.25 CAN 235 EARLY OCT CC 02461
APPROVED BY THE COMICS CODE AUTHORITY

MARVEL® ©1989 MARVEL ENT. GROUP, INC.
$1.00 US $1.25 CAN 241 FEB CC 02461
APPROVED BY THE COMICS CODE AUTHORITY

MARVEL® ©1988 MARVEL ENT. GROUP, INC.
$1.50 US $2.00 CAN 242 MAR CC 02461
APPROVED BY THE COMICS CODE AUTHORITY

MARVEL® ©1989 MARVEL ENT. GROUP, INC.
$1.00 US $1.25 CAN 243 APR CC 02461
APPROVED BY THE COMICS CODE AUTHORITY

MARVEL® ©1989 MARVEL ENT. GROUP, INC.
$1.00 US $1.25 CAN 248 SEPT CC 02461
APPROVED BY THE COMICS CODE AUTHORITY